(2nd copy)    P.   WK

# ON ENGLISHING THE BIBLE

RONALD A. KNOX

# ON
# ENGLISHING
# THE BIBLE

LONDON

BURNS OATES

1949

REVERENDO PATRI RONALDO COX
AMICUS TOTIUS ORBIS SPATIO DIVISUS
SED NOMINE SED STUDIO
MIRUM QUAM VICINUS

NIHIL OBSTAT: EDVARDVS CAN. MAHONEY, S.T.D.
CENSOR DEPVTATVS
IMPRIMATVR: E. MORROGH BERNARD
VICARIVS GENERALIS
WESTMONASTERII: DIE XXVI FEBRVARII MCMXLIX

PRINTED IN GREAT BRITAIN BY HUNT, BARNARD AND CO., LTD.
FOR BURNS OATES & WASHBOURNE LTD.
28 ASHLEY PLACE, LONDON, S.W.1
*First published* 1949

# PREFACE

'WRAGG is in custody.' So ended a newspaper paragraph, in the sixties of last century, about a case of child-murder at Nottingham; and it was not difficult for Matthew Arnold to arraign the industrialized society which turned the wretched heroine of such a tragedy into a bare surname. You may achieve this effect of mononymity without getting into trouble with the police; you can translate the Bible. The thing, I confess, took me by surprise. All my life I had been indifferent to the use of titles; complete strangers referred to me, sometimes in my hearing, as 'Ronnie Knox'—if anything, it was the surname that was regarded as optional. Then I published a translation of the New Testament, and all at once I found I had gone back to my school-days; I was simply 'Knox'. Moffatt said this, Knox said that; I had become one of these translator-fellows.

Let not this depersonalization be confused with fame. Not fame overtakes a Bradshaw, a Whittaker, a Baedeker; the man has turned into a book, has lost (like Wragg) the semblance of humanity; all may speak their minds freely of him, without fear of libel, thenceforward. The odd thing is, a corresponding fixation takes place in the author himself. You may say what you like about *him*; you may not criticize the book with which his name is identified, on pain of an angry rejoinder. I have long since given up protesting when controversialists misquote me, or newspaper columnists credit me with the authorship of Limericks that are none of mine. But if you question a rendering of mine in the New Testament, you come up against a parental instinct hardly less ferocious than that of the mother-bear. I shall smile it off, no doubt, in conversation, but you have lost marks.

And yet, heaven knows, I ought by now to be accustomed to it. All the time I was translating the New Testament, my work was being revised by a committee of experts, briefed by myself to pick holes in it. Then I brought out a trial edition, imploring the general public to contribute its remarks, which meant new corrections here, there and everywhere. For some reason, when the authorized edition was at last produced, I fell to imagining that the voice of criticism would be silent; as if you could ever achieve the perfect compromise, or satisfy the beasts of Ephesus by throwing sops to them! Of course some people will hate what I have written; why shouldn't they? All the same, I get much more angry with the people who like me and don't like my Bible, than with the people who like my Bible and don't like me.

It is a humiliating reflection, that a careful perusal of the holy Scriptures should engender (or perhaps reveal) in one's character this unreasonable streak of touchiness. I can only comfort myself with the thought that, among all the canonized Saints, none has been more frequently accused of touchiness than St. Jerome. Be the reason what it may, I have not always maintained that silence which becomes an author in face of his critics. I would turn round and hit back, generally in the pages of the *Clergy Review*, that admirable safety-valve by which a sorely harassed profession throws off its ill humours. At least I would make it clear to the public what I was trying to do; at least they should know what it was all about. Let them tell me that I had succeeded in ruining the Bible, not that I had failed in the attempt to make a pretty-pretty job of it.

But a further explanation is needed. I may be told that it was all very well to throw off an article, now and again, about Bible translation; by-products of the process, sparks from my anvil; but why republish them? It is an obvious criticism, but one which finds me still impenitent. I am inclined to think that a book of this sort has more permanent value than any translation I have done, or could do. The work of translating the Bible, really translating it, is being taken in hand in our day for the first time since Coverdale. Moffatt and Goodspeed began it, with their fearless challenge of the Authorized Version; their work has been followed up by a text issued with official sanction in the United States. Quite recently, the proposal for a new rendering has been gaining ground among non-Catholics in our own country. Meanwhile, the Catholic hierarchy in the States has entrusted a large body of Biblical scholars with a similar commission. They began with caution; their New Testament was merely a revision, with certain verbal alterations, of the Douay. The Old Testament, to judge by the single volume of it which has so far appeared, is on a far more ambitious scale. They seem resolved, if I may put it in that way, to out-Knox Knox in baldness of narrative and modernity of diction. The germ is spreading, and there will be more translations yet. Indeed, it is doubtful whether we shall ever again allow ourselves to fall under the spell of a single, uniform text, consecrated by its antiquity. And as each new adventurer sets out on his quest for that North-West Passage, the perfect rendering of Holy Writ, he will do well to take note of buoys that mark the channel. Let him ask, not how I did the thing, but how I thought the thing ought to be done. Often he will disagree, but his own ideas will be clarified, none the less, by the effort of disagreement.

In one respect, however—the complaint is general—I have taken my stand upon tradition. The text which my version follows, and, wherever a clear lead is given, the interpretation which it follows, must be sought in the Vulgate; that is, in the primitive Latin rendering of the Scriptures, as revised in the fourth century by St Jerome. This is the text officially used by the Church; and although Rome has recently given us a quite new Psalter, it is not likely that the Vulgate as a whole will be dethroned from its position of privilege within my lifetime. I should be very far indeed from claiming that the Vulgate gives you, everywhere, an accurate interpretation of its original. But you must have a standard text; and the Vulgate Latin is so imbedded in our liturgy and in all our ecclesiastical language that a serious departure from it causes infinite confusion. Meanwhile, the discrepancies between the Vulgate and the (long since abandoned) *textus receptus* are not really as disconcerting as my critics pretend. Where they are slight, they mostly get ironed out in the process of translation; where they are grave, the passage is usually of such difficulty that a footnote would have been demanded in any case. More than once, I have taken refuge in an ambiguous phrase, to by-pass the difficulty.

Here, then, are eight interludes in the business of translation, eight attempts to think aloud while I was doing it. The first has never been published in full; it was a paper read to the Conference of Higher Studies (which met that year at Upholland). The article on Bishop Challoner was contributed to a memorial volume brought out by the *Westminster Cathedral Chronicle*. The short talk which I have labelled *Nine Years' Hard* was given recently on Radio Eireann. The remaining contents of the book are reprinted from the *Clergy Review*. To the editor of that periodical, whose friendship I have now enjoyed for half a life-time, and to those who sponsored the first appearance of the other essays, I take this opportunity of expressing my gratitude.

And not only to them, but to many others in many lands who have written to express appreciation of what I had done, and encouraged me to hope that, so far as human praise was worth having, I had not run in vain. May they be rewarded for all the pleasure, and pardoned for all the feelings of self-importance, which their delicate kindness has provoked.

MELLS, 1949.                          R. A. KNOX.

# CONTENTS

# THOUGHTS ON BIBLE
# TRANSLATION [1]

Almost for the first time in my life, I am reading a paper
before a learned audience *con amore*. As a rule, I find the
process involves talking about something in which you
are not interested, talking about something of which you
have no knowledge, or talking about something about
which there is very little to say—sometimes all three.
*Now*, all I have got to do is to ventilate the ideas which
have been simmering in my brain continuously these last
three years; the ideas which, unless I am carefully con-
trolled, I pour out freely in conversation. There is a
great deal to be said about translating the Bible; most of
that I claim to know, even if I know nothing else, and I
am furiously interested in it.

Let us be precise; when I talk about translating the
Bible, I mean translating the Vulgate. I have every respect
for the patient scholarship which is giving us the West-
minster Version, and I have sometimes found myself
envying its compilers their liberty. But, it is well known,
for all official purposes a Bible translation must take the
Vulgate as its standard. I have been translating, these last
three years, from the Vulgate text, relegating other read-
ings, however plausible, to the foot of the page. I have
even denied myself the privilege claimed by the latest
American revisers, of going back behind the Clementine
edition, and taking the Vulgate as it stands (say) in
Wordsworth and White's collation of it. The American

[1] A paper read to the Catholic Conference of Higher Studies.

version, for example, in Acts xvii. 6, has 'these men who are setting the world in an uproar'. That is quite certainly the true reading; but a bad copyist has written *urbem* instead of *orbem*, and the Clementine follows this tradition. So I have rendered, 'who turn the state upside down'; that is how the thing stands in every Vulgate in the world nowadays, and it is no part of the translator's business to alter, on however good grounds, his original.

That is not to say, that when you are translating a translation you must never look back at the original document. There will be passages in which the Latin is patient of two different interpretations; and here the original will put you right. This is especially true in the Vulgate psalms; only the original to which you must refer is not the Hebrew but the Septuagint, which they follow almost slavishly. Again, there will be passages in which the Latin translators have thrown up the sponge, and simply given you a meaningless transliteration of the Greek; in Acts xvii. 18, for example, the word *spermologos* is translated *seminiverbius*. You cannot translate *seminiverbius*; it is a *vox nihili*. If the Vulgate had meant 'one who sows words', it would have given us *sator verborum*. In such a case, I hold, the English translator is justified in going back to the Greek, and giving the most accurate rendering of it that he can find. Much oftener, the Latin gives you a weak equivalent for a colourful word in the original; thus, in the first passage I have alluded to, *concito*, to stir up, is a very weak rendering of *anastatoo*, to turn a thing upside down. Here (though with less confidence) I claim the right to go back to the original, and render, 'turn the state upside down', because *concito* does not contradict that notion, and is not meant to contradict it; it simply falls short of it.

The only considerable liberty I have allowed myself of

going back behind the Latin—and I have only done so tentatively—is to restore, here and there, more plausible tenses to the verbs when the Latin comes, directly or indirectly, from the Hebrew. In the psalms, particularly, [1] I do not see how you are to make any consecutive sense of passages here and there unless you give a present where the Latin has a perfect, and sometimes where the Latin has a future. King David had, after all, only two tenses to express himself in; and by the time the Septuagint has translated his imperfect (or was it a future?) into an aorist which may or may not be gnomic, and the Vulgate has translated the aorist into a perfect which may or may not be the 'perfect with have', a rich confusion has been introduced into the time-sequence which impels the translator to put the verb in the present and call it a day. You must, after all, translate with some reference to the context.

That, then, is what we have to translate—the Clementine recension of the Vulgate. And now, how are we to translate it?

Two alternatives present themselves at once, the literal and the literary method of translation. Is it to be 'Arms and the man I sing', or is it to be something which will pass for English? If you are translating for the benefit of a person who wants to learn Latin by following the gospel in a Latin missal when it is read out in church, then your 'Arms and the man I sing' is exactly what he wants. If you are translating for the benefit of a person who wants to be able to read the word of God for ten minutes on end without laying it aside in sheer boredom or bewilderment, a literary translation is what you want—and we have been lacking it for centuries.

Among the many good things Mr. Belloc has done

[1]This was written before the appearance of the new Latin psalter.

which are almost entirely unknown, is a little brochure
of 44 pages, the substance of a lecture he once gave at the
Taylorian, on 'Translation'. The great principle he there
lays down is that the business of a translator is not to ask,
'How shall I make this foreigner talk English?' but 'What
would an Englishman have said to express this?' For instance, he says, if you are faced with the French sentence,
'Il y avait dans cet homme je ne sais quoi de suffisance',
you do not want to write, 'There was in this man I know
not what of self-sufficiency'; you want to write, 'There
was a touch of complacency about him'. So with 'Arms
and the man'. You have not translated the phrase when
you have merely corrected the preposterous order, and
written, 'I sing of arms and the man'. 'Sing' is only used
like that by English poets when they are imitating Virgil,
and you must not translate Virgil by imitating Virgil. The
opening is also too abrupt; there is not time to give the
words 'I sing' a proper emphasis. You want something
like, 'My song tells of arms; tells of the man', and so on.
Anybody who has really tackled the business of translation, at least where the classical languages are concerned,
will tell you that the bother is not finding the equivalent
for this or that word, it is finding out how to turn the
sentence. And about this, the older translators of the
Bible took no trouble at all. Take this sentence: 'The
Pharisees, and all the Jews, except they wash their hands
oft, eat not, holding the tradition of the elders'. No, do
not exclaim against the cumbrousness of Douay; that
comes from the Authorized Version. The Authorized
Version is supposed to be the fountain of pure English;
but there it gives you an English sentence which would
get any man the sack, and rightly, from Fleet Street. 'For
the Pharisees, and indeed all the Jews, holding to the
tradition of their ancestors, never eat without washing

their hands again and again'—there is the English of
it.

Incidentally, let us never be taken in by the people who
talk to us about the 'effective inversions of order' which
bring out the emphasis so well in the Bible. There are,
indeed, such things as effective inversions of order. But
what they mean is a sentence like, 'If I by the finger of
God cast out devils'. Here, the operative words, 'by the
finger of God', have been taken away from the end of the
sentence, where the emphasis would have fallen on them,
and shipped round to the front, leaving the whole emphasis of the sentence wrong; 'If I by the finger of God
cast out DEVILS', as if somebody had been accusing our
Lord of casting out angels. There, of course, the Authorized Version knew better; it was Douay, feverishly keep-
ing the order of the Latin, that gave us the piece of false
rhetoric to which our ears, by annual repetition, have
grown accustomed.

I say, then, that the first thing demanded of a new
translation of the Vulgate is that it should break away
from the literal translation of sentences. What could be
flatter than the first verse of St. John, as usually translated, 'In the beginning was the Word, and the Word
was with God, and the Word was God'? That represents
a very subtle chiasmus in the Greek, closely followed by
the Latin; 'Et Verbum erat apud Deum, et Deus erat
Verbum'. To restore that chiasmus, you must have something like 'God had the Word abiding with him, and the
Word was God'. Latin and Greek leave the end of the
sentence unemphatic, English emphasizes the end of the
sentence. Therefore the English for 'De tribu Juda duo-
decim millia signati' is not what we are accustomed to.
It is, 'Twelve thousand were sealed of the tribe of JUDA'.
You must play cat's cradle with almost every sentence in

the New Testament, if you want to decide *how an English-man would have said the same thing*.

So much for sentences; and now, what of phrases? It stands to reason that no two languages have exactly the same idiom; that the English for 'Comment vous portez-vous?' is not 'How do you carry yourself?' If anybody has come across that extremely rare book, 'English as she is Spoke', he will know what I mean. The book was a phrase-book compiled by a Portuguese author for the benefit of English travellers in Portugal. And you do not need much critical insight to detect the fact that this well-meaning gentleman knew no English at all. He knew French; so he translated his sentences into French and then did them into English with a dictionary. Consequently, when he wanted to render a Portuguese idiom which meant, 'to wait about, to kick one's heels', he could do all right for the first part of his process; he knew that the corresponding idiom in French was 'croquer le marmot'—I have no notion why. The English, therefore, for kicking one's heels was 'to crunch the marmoset'. It is an extremely entertaining book; but, if you come to think of it, practically every translation of the Bible you have ever read makes errors which are quite as ludicrous—only we are accustomed to them. Douay was consistent; it translated the Latin word for word, and if you protested that its version sounded rather odd, replied woodenly, 'Well, that's what it says'. In the eleventh psalm, for instance, you get the words 'Deceitful lips, they have spoken in heart and heart'. Even Challoner saw that that would not do, so he pillaged from the Author-ized Version and gave us 'With a double heart have they spoken'. I don't see what a double heart could be except an abnormal anatomical condition, or an obscure kind of convention at bridge; but anyhow it sounds a little more like English. But when the Latin had 'Renew a right spirit within my bowels', that was what Challoner put; and when the Latin had 'Examine, O Lord, my kidneys', Challoner put that down too; only he changed kidneys to the obsolete word 'reins', hoping that his readers would not look it up in the dictionary. We are sensible of these Hebraisms, and most of us would like to see the last of them. But there are hundreds and hundreds of other Hebraisms which we do not notice, because we have allowed ourselves to grow accustomed to them. We should have thought it odd if we had read in *The Times*, 'General Montgomery's right hand has smitten Rommel in the hinder parts'; but if we get that sort of thing in the Bible we take it, unlike Rommel, sitting down. 'Mr. Churchill then opened his mouth and spoke'—is that English? No, it is Hebrew idiom clothed in English words.

Constantly, then, you have to be on the look-out for phrases which, because you have so often met them in the Bible, read like English, and yet are not English. Many of them, beginning life as Bible English, have even crept into the language; 'to give a person the right hand of fellow-ship', for example, or 'to sleep with one's fathers', or 'the son of perdition'; if the translator is not careful, he will let these through the barrier by mistake, and he will be wrong. When a public speaker urges that we should give Chiang Kai-shek the right hand of fellowship, he *means* 'give him the right hand of fellowship, as the dear old Bible would say'. And when you are translating the Bible, you must not describe the apostles as 'giving Paul and Barnabas the right hand of fellowship, as the dear old Bible would say'. Some of the phrases which we take over, as unconscious quotations, from the Authorized Version, or more rarely from Douay, have even become

B

jocose. It is intolerable, in a modern translation of the New Testament, to find St. Paul talking about 'the inner man', when 'the inner man' has been used for so many years as a facetious synonym for the human stomach. If you are simply revising the old text of the Douay, you may, perhaps, be justified in leaving such phrases as they stand. But if you are writing a translation of the Bible, a translation of your own, you must find some other way of putting it; 'the inner man' is a phrase that has become desecrated.

Apropos of that, may I suggest some considerations about what are called 'consecrated phrases' in the Bible, which, we are told, we must not alter in any way, because they have become so familiar? I quite admit that where a form of words has become stereotyped through passing into liturgical use, it is a pity and probably a waste of time to try and alter it. The words of the *Our Father* and of the *Hail Mary* have got to remain as they are. Again, there are certain formulas which are best left alone, or altered as little as possible, because alteration cannot hope to make them clearer, and they have already a supreme literary value of their own, depending on association; the words of Consecration, for example, or the seven words from the Cross. But it is, I submit, a grave error to stick to a form of words, in itself unnatural English, merely because a thousand repetitions have familiarized the public ear with the sound of it. Just because we are familiar with a form of words, we fail to be struck by its full meaning. For instance, I had a very interesting letter from an Irish Redemptorist, expressing the hope that I had found some better translation for *arneito heauton* (*abneget semetipsum*) than 'Let him deny himself'. This has become a consecrated phrase, and for years, now, nuns have been encouraging schoolgirls to give up toffee during Lent and write the fact down on a card as a record of 'self-denial'. For years, Salvation Army lasses have picketed us with demands for a half-penny because it is 'self-denial week'. The whole glorious content of the phrase, *arneito heauton*, let him obliterate himself, let him annihilate himself, let him rule Self out of his world-picture altogether, has become degraded and lost. That is what happens to 'consecrated phrases'.

I have urged that the translator's business is to recondition, as often as not, whole sentences, so as to allow for the characteristic emphasis of his own language. I have urged that it is his business to transpose whole phrases, so as to reduce them to the equivalent idiom of his own language. And now, what of words? Here a consideration comes which is often forgotten. The Bible is usually translated by a syndicate; and the first thing a syndicate does when it gets together is to make sure that all the members of it tell the same story. If you proposed to translate the Aeneid in this way, each member of it translating one book, the first item on the Committee's agenda would be, What is going to be our formula for translating the word *pius* as applied to the hero of the poem? They go away, after agreeing (say) on the word 'dutiful', which does well enough. But if a single man translates the whole Aeneid, he very soon realizes that *pius* takes on a different shade of meaning with each fresh context; now it is 'Aeneas, that dutiful son', now it is 'Aeneas, that admirable host', now it is 'Aeneas, that trained liturgiologist'. The compilers of the Authorized Version evidently did something of that kind with a word like *dikaiosune* in the New Testament, or *tsedeq* in the Old. They could see that Douay's rendering, 'justice', was beside the mark nine times out of ten. What they did was to resuscitate a more or less obsolete word, 'right-wiseness', recondition it as 'righteousness', and use that all through the Bible as the equivalent of the *tsedeq-dikaiosune* idea. It served well enough; but this wooden rendering, constantly recurring in all sorts of different contexts, has resulted all through the Authorized Version in a certain flatness, a certain want of grip. You constantly feel that your author is not being allowed to say what he wants to say; his thought is being forced into an artificial mould.

For every common word in every living language has, not one meaning, but a quantity of shades of meaning. If you set out to give *salus* the meaning of 'salvation' all through the New Testament, you find yourself up against St. Paul inviting the ship's company during the storm to take a little food for the sake of their salvation. It is a capital heresy among translators, the idea that you must *always* render so-and-so in Latin by such-and-such in English. We sometimes get the idea that this must be a holy principle; is it not, after all, we are asked, the way in which the Vulgate proceeds in translating the Greek of the New Testament? If anybody harbours that delusion, he is recommended to consult Plummer's edition of II Corinthians; he will find there an appendix giving about 250 Greek words in the epistles, each of which the Vulgate renders in two or more ways. The word *eudokein*, he points out, is rendered in no less than ten different ways in the epistles alone. He appears to be scandalized by this procedure, which shows that he knew very little about translation. It is true, I think, that the Vulgate very often picks on the *wrong* rendering, the word with the wrong shade of meaning for that particular context. Over that, Plummer is welcome to have a grievance. But let him not demand that *eudokein* should be translated 'be well pleased' wherever it occurs, simply for the sake of uniformity.

Words are not coins, dead things whose value can be mathematically computed. You cannot quote an exact English equivalent for a French word, as you might quote an exact English equivalent for a French coin. Words are living things, full of shades of meaning, full of associations; and, what is more, they are apt to change their significance from one generation to the next. The translator who understands his job feels, constantly, like Alice in Wonderland trying to play croquet with flamingoes for mallets and hedgehogs for balls; words are for ever eluding his grasp. Think of the delicate differences there are between the shades of meaning in a group of words like 'mercy, pity, clemency, pardon', or a group of words like 'fear, terror, awe, reverence, respect', or a group of words like 'glory, honour, fame, praise, credit'. How is it to be expected, on the law of averages, that any such group of words in English has an exactly corresponding group of words in Latin, and another in Greek, so that you can say, for example, *doxa* always means *gloria* in Latin, always means 'glory' in English? *Tsedeq* or *dikaiosune* can mean, when used of a man, innocence, or honesty, or uprightness, or charitableness, or dutifulness, or (very commonly) the fact of being in God's good books. Used of God, it can mean the justice which punishes the sinner, or, quite as often, the faithfulness which protects the good; it can mean, also, the approval with which God looks upon those who are in his good books. Only a meaningless token-word, like righteousness, can pretend to cover all these meanings. To use such a token-word is to abrogate your duty as a translator. Your duty as a translator is to think up the right expression, though it may have to be a paraphrase, which will give the reader the exact shade of meaning *here* and *here* and *here*.

The translator, let me suggest in passing, must never be frightened of the word 'paraphrase'; it is a bogey of the half-educated. As I have already tried to point out, it is almost impossible to translate a *sentence* without paraphrasing; it is a paraphrase when you translate 'Comment vous portez-vous?' by 'How are you?' But often enough it will be a single word that calls for paraphrase. When St. Paul describes people as 'wise according to the flesh', the translator is under an obligation to paraphrase. In English speech, you might be called fat according to the flesh, or thin according to the flesh, but not wise or foolish. The flesh here means natural, human standards of judging, and the translator has got to say so. 'Wise according to the flesh' is Hebrew in English dress; it is not English. You have not translated 'Galeotto fu il libro, e chi lo scrisse', if you write, 'The book was Galahad, and so was the man who wrote it'. Dante's 'Galeotto' (being paraphrased) means 'a pandar'; and how (shades of Lord Tennyson!) is the English reader to know that?

The sentence, the phrase, the word—over all these the translator must keep watch; must beware of the instinct which bids him save trouble, or avoid criticism, by giving a merely photographic reproduction of his original. Nor does his task end there; his matter has to be duly chopped up into sentences. The first sentence of St. Paul's epistle to the Romans has ninety-one Latin words in it. The second sentence in his epistle to the Ephesians has a hundred and eighty-two. I admit that these figures are exceptional, but it is the clear fact about St. Paul that he thought in paragraphs. St. John, on the other hand, has an insatiable passion for full stops. And nothing,

I fancy, is so subtly disconcerting to the modern reader as having his intellectual food cut up into unsuitable lengths. The easy art of making it masticable has been learned to perfection by the journalists and public speakers whose thought he is accustomed to follow. If you want him to read Scripture without a kind of unconscious indigestion, you must prepare it more or less according to the current formula.

'The modern reader,' I have said; thereby, I am afraid, taking for granted a point which remains to be discussed. Ought the modern reader of the Bible to have the illusion that he is reading something written in the twentieth century? Or will he prefer to have these holy documents wrapped up in archaic forms, just as he prefers to see the priest at Mass dressed up in a sixth-century overcoat? The latter suggestion is not so improbable as it sounds. Unlike the French, the English have always been accustomed to having an archaic Bible. Douay and the Authorized Version were compiled in the time of Shakespeare; but neither was written in the idiom of Shakespeare's time. Read a couple of pages out of any of the comedies, and you will be sensible of it at once. More than three centuries have passed, and as current idiom has changed, 'Bible English' has become a sort of hieratic language; it is old, therefore it is venerable (for it is a fixed belief in the heart of the ordinary Englishman that the word 'venerable' means 'old'). Let him beware, then, who proposes to alter it. Let him try to render the sense of Scripture plainer to us by whatever means he will, but let him adhere (or rather, let him cleave) to the good old-fashioned diction which was good enough for our forefathers, and is still better for us because for us it is still more old-fashioned.

Upon my word, if I had been trying to translate the

Bible a hundred years ago, or even at the time when it seemed as if Newman was to be entrusted with the work of translating the Bible, these arguments would have impressed me. For England, and indeed Europe generally, was then passing through a phase of romantic revival, and all our art and literature reeked of the past. Pugin, erecting Gothic cathedrals while you waited, Rossetti and Burne Jones covering yards of canvas with Arthurian legends executed in the very manner of Fra Angelico, William Morris pouring out synthetic medievalism, and all the poets, from Keats to Tennyson, dredging the Faery Queen to get hold of more and more odd words to impress the British public with—ah, it would have been child's play translating the Bible then! I believe I would have executed a version of the Scriptures, compared to which the old Douay would have looked painfully modern, and almost colloquial. But that was a hundred or nearly a hundred years ago.

To-day, we have boxed the compass. Rightly or wrongly, architecture is breaking away everywhere from the Gothic tradition. Our artists, instead of boasting themselves pre-Raphaelite, are looking round all the time to see what they can be Post. Poets speak in the language of the day, often in the strong language of the day. Prose-writers produce remarkable effects by breaking suddenly into italics, and filling their pages up with rows and rows of little dots. The young men will criticize Stevenson for caring so much about style, as if style mattered! The most damning criticism which can be passed on any work of art is that it is bogus; and how can any literature fail to be bogus that is deliberately written in the manner of four hundred years ago? Whatever else our contemporaries may worship, they will not bow the knee to the past; we have debunked the past.

Am I, then, prepared to haul down my colours, and pipe to this generation in the airs it has grown accustomed to, in the hope that it will dance? Must I translate the Bible in the idiom of James Joyce, or of Louis Macneice? I confess that I draw a different moral from the disconcerting change of fashion which I have been trying, very inadequately, to outline. It seems to me that elderly people, among whose number I am reluctantly beginning to reckon myself, have lived through enough vicissitudes of public taste to beware of catering exclusively for the mood of to-day. If the conventions of art can, in our times, be so rapidly overhauled, catering for the mood of to-day will mean, almost certainly, ministering to the nausea of to-morrow. The moral, surely, is that anybody who tries to do a new translation of the Bible in these days should aim at producing something which will not, in fifty or a hundred years' time, be 'dated'. In a word, what you want is neither sixteenth-century English nor twentieth-century English, but timeless English. Whether you can get it, is another question. The method I proposed to myself was this—to use no word, no phrase, and as far as possible no turn of sentence, which would not have passed as decent literary English in the seventeenth century, and would not pass as decent literary English to-day. All these last three years, Murray's dictionary, in the full-size edition, has been more frequently in my hands than Forcellini, or Liddell and Scott, or Gesenius.

Strictly speaking, the thing is not possible. 'Peter stood at the door without' sounds old-fashioned to-day; 'Peter stood at the door outside' would have been incomprehensible in the seventeenth century. And I confess that I have preserved one or two archaisms; 'multitude', for example—'crowd' is such an ugly word; and 'brethren', so familiar in ecclesiastical use, and one or two others. Much more serious was the problem, what to do about 'thou' and 'you'. I confess I would have liked to go the whole hog, and dispense with the use of 'thou' and 'thee', even where the Almighty was being addressed. They do these things in France, but I felt sure you could not get it past the British public. Why not, then, have 'thou' for God and 'you' for man? That is Moffatt's principle; but it seems to me to break down hopelessly in relation to our Incarnate Lord. Who is to say, exactly, when he is being addressed as God and when he is being addressed as Man? Moffatt makes St. Paul address him as 'you' in a vision, but the Lamb of the Apocalypse is 'thou'. In a single chapter of the Hebrews, quoting from a single psalm, Moffatt gives us 'thou art my Son', and 'sit at my right hand till I make your enemies a foot-stool'. I despaired in the face of these difficulties, and resolved to keep 'thou', with its appropriate forms, throughout, at the same time abolishing third-person forms like 'speaketh', which serve no useful purpose whatever.

On the other hand, I confess that I have given more weight to modern usage in certain points; particularly over the conjunctions at the beginning of sentences or clauses. The conjunction, it seems to me, is tending to disappear. Nobody, nowadays, uses 'therefore' at the beginning of a sentence. We say, 'I must be going, I've got to catch a 'bus', not 'I must be going, for I've got to catch a 'bus'. No modern crowd would shout, 'Not this man, but Barabbas'; it would be, 'Not this man; Barabbas!' And I confess that I think our language is gaining in strength by depending more on emphasis, less on subsidiary parts of speech. Here, if nowhere else, I have confessed myself a child of the twentieth century.

I cannot guess what impression all these considerations will make on my audience; I only know that when I set them out like this, they convince *me*. But I am not, for that, too sanguine in the belief that anything will be done about giving us a new translation of the Bible—I mean, for official purposes. If such a step is proposed, I am quite sure that it will meet with opposition from a number of influential people—almost all of them priests— who will be honestly convinced that the Catholic public is being deprived of a priceless possession. We shall be told about the simple folk, always invoked on such occasions, who like what they have always been accustomed to. The faith of our grandfathers will be mentioned a great deal, and nothing will be said about the faith of our grandchildren. It is easy to organize opposition, where the discomforts attendant on a change will be felt by the clergy of to-day, while the benefits are for the clergy of to-morrow.

And yet, is the Douay, as it has come down to us through Challoner, really so familiar to us, so universally beloved? I understand that for several years, during and after the war, it was impossible, in England or Scotland, for a Catholic to buy a copy of the New Testament. Would any other Christian denomination in the world have sat down under that? In my experience, the laity's attitude towards the Bible is one of blank indifference, varied now and again by one of puzzled hostility. The clergy, no doubt, search the Scriptures more eagerly. And yet, when I used to go round preaching a good deal, and would ask the P.P. for a Bible to verify my text from, there was generally an ominous pause of twenty minutes or so before he returned, banging the leaves of the sacred volume and visibly blowing on the top. The new wine of the gospel, you felt, was kept in strangely cobwebby bottles.

No doubt certain passages, familiarized to us by being

read out on solemn occasions—St. John's account of the Passion, for example—have entwined themselves graciously in the memory. But let anyone take up the Douay version and open it at random in the middle of the epistles; what does he make of the strange by-paths of it? Take this passage, for example, from the Hebrews. 'For the priesthood being translated, it is necessary that a translation also be made of the law. For he of whom these things are spoken is of another tribe, of which no one attended on the altar. For it is evident that our Lord sprang out of Juda: in which tribe Moses spoke nothing concerning priests. And it is yet far more evident: if according to the similitude of Melchisedech there ariseth another priest, who is made, not according to the law of a carnal commandment, but according to the power of an indissoluble life.' My ear may be faulty, but I do not find anything very impressive about the cadences I have just read; and as for the *meaning*—one knows the *sort* of thing it means, because one has read it in the Latin; but as a piece of English it is gibberish; you can give it no other name. The Douay people knew how to write, and Challoner's age was an age in which men could give you a good rendering—witness that extract from an old version Fr. Hugh Pope sent me, from the epistle of St. James, 'And he says to the fine suit of clothes, Sit you here, that's for quality'; there you have translation. But the Bible translated at Douay on the principle of Kelly's Keys, and then watered down by Challoner to make it sound less rugged—was there any hope that this would give us desirable English?

# II

# SOME NEW TESTAMENT PROBLEMS

'TRANSMUTE boldly: render the sense by the corresponding sense without troubling over the verbal difficulties in your way. Where such rendering of sense by corresponding sense involves considerable amplification, do not hesitate to amplify for fear of being verbose . . . Sometimes, even, a whole passage must be thus transmuted, a whole paragraph thrown into a new form, if we would justly render the sense of the original; and the rule should stand that, after having grasped as exactly as possible all that the original stands for, with the proportion between its various parts, the distinction between what is emphasized and what is left on a lower plane, we should say to ourselves, not "How shall I make this foreigner talk English?" but "What would an Englishman have said to express the same?" *That* is translation. *That* is the very essence of the art: the resurrection of an alien thing in a native body; not the dressing of it up in native clothes but the giving to it of native flesh and blood.'

So Mr. Belloc told us, in a lecture he gave at the Taylorian in 1931. Is it any use to remember these principles, or ought they to be expunged ruthlessly from the mind, when you sit down to translate inspired documents for the benefit of a conservative public bred chiefly on texts, under the eye of a censor who has never reflected that the word *concordat* is derived from *cor*? Certainly there is no official translation of the Bible known to me which does not abandon, from the start, the dream of preserving its native idiom, which does not resign itself, from the start, to being a word-for-word translation. It is no use objecting that the Authorized Version is good English. The Authorized Version is good English only because English writers, for centuries, have treated it as the standard of good English. In itself, it is no better English than the Douay; Professor Phillimore used to maintain that the Douay was better. Only the Douay was written in the language of exiles, which became, with time, an exiled language. Lately, a generation which has revolted against the domination of the Old Masters has shown signs of revolting against Authorized Version English. But whatever comes of that, it remains true that the Authorized Version is essentially a word-for-word translation, no less than the Septuagint, no less than the Vulgate.

Let me commit to paper some of the hesitations which make themselves felt when you sit down, trying to forget that you have ever read the Bible before, to contemplate a verse of the Vulgate, with the Greek printed on the opposite side of the page, and ask yourself, What is the English for this?

To begin with, every language has its obscurities; has words which do duty for two different meanings. The word 'blood', for example, has two quite different meanings in the two sentences, 'Blood will tell', and 'He is out for blood'. In the same way, neither Hebrew nor Greek nor Latin has two separate words for 'earth', in the sense of the terrestrial globe, and 'land' in the sense of a particular region of it. When we are told that there was darkness over all the *terra* at the time of our Lord's Crucifixion, how are we to know whether that darkness was world-wide, or was only noticeable in Palestine? The Greek does not help us; it would not help us if we had access to the original Aramaic of St. Matthew. In translating such a verse you must accept the responsibility for creating this or that impression in the minds of (you hope) innumerable readers, of whom only one in ten ever looks at a footnote. It is the same with *gratia*; like *charis*, it may mean 'grace' or it may mean 'favour'. The Douay plays for safety; but is there really any sense in saying that our Lord grew in grace with men? And a similar difficulty arises over the printing of 'spirit' with or without a capital S, in a verse like Matthew iv. 1 ('led by the spirit into the wilderness'); the old Douay had the courage to print 'Word' with a capital W in the second verse of St. Luke. You cannot be a translator without being, to some extent, an interpreter; and the ways of the Catholic interpreter are not always plain or easy.

What obligation is there, again, of following St. Jerome's rendering of the Greek, when his meaning appears to differ from that of the Greek? I say, 'appears'; in some case the appearance is quite illusory. For example, why did the Wise Men receive an 'answer' in sleep? Why did Simeon receive an 'answer' from the Holy Ghost that he should see the Christ? There is no suggestion, in either case, that a question had been asked; and the use of the word is one of those multitudinous touches which afflict the reader of our English Bible with distractions. The solution is very simple; St. Jerome's *responsum* does not mean an answer. It means an oracle; it is a technical word for an oracle. The Greek had used *chrematizomai*, and St. Jerome, in his strict preference for verbal equivalents, did the best he could to give the oracular atmosphere without using the pagan word *oraculum*. The Douay, therefore, is translating a shade of meaning which is not there. The nearest you can get to the sense is, 'a revelation'.

The same sort of confusion arises in a much more serious context. One of the leading differences between

the Catholic and the Protestant Bible is that the former
gives 'do penance' (from *poenitentiam agere*) where the
latter gives 'repent' (from *metanoein*). Rivers of ink
flowed over the controversy; Catholic expositors were
determined not to let it be supposed that sins were for-
given in return for a mere attitude of the mind, as
opposed to a genuine alteration of the will. Perhaps, too,
they were anxious to assert the principle of reparation,
though here they had less support from the Greek.
Challoner has kept to the old rendering; Lingard, in the
new conditions of a Victorian world, not only adopts
'repent', but sets store by the change. His admirable
footnote says, 'Though there can be no true repentance
which produces not reformation, there is often a reformation which is not produced by repentance'. Protestant thought has boxed the compass, as usual; to-day,
what it needs to be told is that 'turning over a new leaf'
does not, unless it involves regret, avail to obliterate the
past. And meanwhile, what was the linguistic background
of the whole dispute? Simply that St. Jerome had used
*poenitentiam agere*, and St. Jerome must know. But, in
point of fact, St. Jerome had to use *poenitentiam agere*;
there is no other way of saying 'Repent', since *poenitet*
has to be impersonal, except in the participle.

There are instances, however, in which the Greek
admits of two rival interpretations, whereas the Latin
only allows of one. The word *pais* can mean 'son' or
'servant'; which does it mean in Acts iii. 13? Westcott
and Hort mark the end of the verse as a quotation from
Isaias lii. 13, in which case we ought certainly to render
'servant'. But St. Jerome has *servus* in Isaias, and *filius*
in Acts. If the translator is convinced (which I am not)
that the passage in Acts is a quotation, is he bound to
follow St. Jerome blindfold in an inconsistency? More

annoying, because it is much more common, is the hesitation whether he can be allowed to translate *verbum* 'a thing'. Here the ambiguity goes back behind the Greek; it is *dabhar*, not *rhema*, that does double duty and so creates a confusion. The Douay imitates, of course, Latin and Greek in their literalness. But could the shepherds really have said, 'Let us go to Bethlehem and see this word which has happened?' Does it mean anything?

It is easy to say that the Vulgate must always be followed, because it enshrines Catholic tradition. But this is not always true. Almost any Catholic, if asked whether our Lady stayed with Elizabeth until after St. John was born, would reply, 'Of course she did'. But if he will look in the Vulgate, or in the Douay, he will find that she did not. In the Greek, you can read it either way, since the aorists in Luke i. 37 can legitimately be taken as pluperfect. But St. Jerome represents them as perfects; can the translator go behind St. Jerome here, in order to follow a tradition? Or must he, at best, 'do a straddle'—invent some formula which would fit either interpretation? And can he do that, without ceasing to be literal?

So much for ambiguities. But even where the sense is indisputable, the translator will be conscious that there is a right way and a wrong way of putting things; and the chances are that the literal way will be the wrong way. When Horace writes, *Da, puer, auguris Maecenae*, we expect the phrase to be rendered, 'Fill a bumper, slave, to Maecenas' augurship!'; we conceive that the translator has not done his duty if he is content with, 'Give, boy, of the augur Maecenas'. Yet that is what we should, almost certainly, have got if the words stood in the Bible. We have all grown accustomed to 'they shall not leave in thee a stone upon a stone'; but it is not English. The Jews lacked the useful phrase 'one another'; they had to talk

c

about man-stone being left on his friend. Must we really imitate their poverty of speech, under pain of discordance with the original? There is the same objection to 'feared with a great fear', and 'desiring I have desired'; both locutions are intelligible, but, being quite unnatural English, they make the narrative seem remote, not part of ourselves; some people call it 'dignified'.

Moreover, some idioms when translated into a different language lose all their meaning, and serve to darken interpretation. *Tu dixisti*, for example; evidently the Aramaic form of speech which underlies this was as definite as the modern American, 'You said it'. If you were translating an American novel into French you would not translate 'You said it' by 'Vous l'avez dit'. Are we bound, then, to translate *Tu dixisti* by 'Thou hast said it'? ('Thou hast said' by itself is not even grammar.) To be sure, the faithful mostly know what is meant; they have been told about it in sermons. But why must the Catholic clergy spend so much of their time in explaining that the Bible doesn't mean what it says? . . . In one passage a Hebrew idiom has been obscured by Challoner, who does not even allude to it in his footnote on the passage. When our Lady says, at Cana of Galilee, 'They have no wine', there is no reasonable doubt that our Lord replied, 'Let me alone'; the Jewish idiom for which is, 'What have I to do with thee?' The Protestant Bible, in translating the idiom literally, makes it sound much too harsh. But Challoner has not dared even to be literal; he adopts without comment the far less probable interpretation, 'What is that (the absence of wine) to me and to thee?'

The old Douay, in the same passage, is very illuminating. It gives the translation, 'What is to me and to thee, woman?' without pretending that it is English. And the

footnote says, 'Because this speech is subject to divers
senses, we keep the words of our text, lest by turning it
into any English phrase we might straiten the Holy
Ghost's intention to some certain sense either not intended, or not only intended, and so take away the choice
and indifferency from the reader, whereof (in holy Scripture specially) all translators must beware'. The principle
is one of capital importance; where interpreters disagree, the reader must be given his choice and indifferency as much as possible, though Challoner does not
seem to have thought so. But does that justify the translator in printing gibberish? Ought he not rather, in these
rare cases, to resort to a paraphrase which will be vague
enough to cover both interpretations? 'Do not trouble
me, woman'—something of that kind.

Metaphors, no less than idioms, have their difficulty
for the translator. Sometimes their meaning is trans-
parent enough; the scribes and Pharisees, for example,
'sitting in Moses' seat', although the picture which the
imagination conjures up is one of extreme discomfort.
But is any picture conjured up at all, to the ordinary
English mind, by 'a horn of salvation'? And, if we must
preserve all other metaphors in their exact form, out of
faithfulness to the original, surely it is time we got rid of
'bowels'? Cruden's *Concordance* gives some thirty instances of the word's use, only seven of which have a
literal acceptation; our own version is still more fond of
the idea, which disfigures our translations of the *Miserere*
and of the *Benedictus*. Surely, as a general principle, we do
better justice to the author's meaning when we translate
*viscera* by 'heart' (and *cor* by 'mind')?

There are, besides, certain words of very frequent
occurrence which always strike the wrong note when
you translate them literally from the Latin, because they

are not familiar in the sense intended. 'Just', for example. Even when the connotations of the word are
merely moral, it is not the word we want; the man who
does not steal your umbrella is not 'just', he is 'honest'.
Far more frequently, *justus* in the Vulgate has a strictly
theological sense; under the Old Dispensation the *justus*
is a man who is right with God, because he is careful to
keep the law, moral and ceremonial; under the New
Dispensation he is simply a 'justified' person (e.g.
Romans v. 19). The Protestant translators preferred the
word 'righteous', and the word 'just' has therefore
passed out of English usage in that sense. (At least,
English authors do use it of the dead, as in Vaughan's
'Dear, beauteous death, the jewel of the just'; but I think
he got it from Shirley's 'Only the actions of the just
smell sweet, and blossom in their dust'; and Shirley was
a Catholic.) Take, again, the word 'flesh'. It suggests to
the modern Catholic ear associations of bodily self-
indulgence; but in the New Testament it means, nearly
always, the natural as opposed to the supernatural man,
and especially where his mind is concerned. Or take the
word 'scandal'. To Protestants it means uncharitable
conversation; to Catholics it means setting a bad example. But in the New Testament it means anything
which 'puts you off', creates misgivings in you about the
religious creed which you follow, or tends to do so.

You cannot, without sacrificing clear thought, treat
words like these as mere counters, internationally available; each language gives its own twist to the more inti-
mate ideas it tries to express. Nor can you even, without
sacrificing clearness of thought, use the same equivalent
for the same word in every passage where it occurs. 'Thou
art a scandal unto me,' 'Whosoever shall scandalize one
of these little ones,' 'All you shall be scandalized because

of me this night'—you cannot find a single English word which will fit all those three passages; except 'scandal', which is not, in any of the three passages, recognizable English.

And then there is the coupling of sentences . . . There are nearly a hundred 'ands' in the first chapter of Genesis, about fifty in the first chapter of St. Matthew, eighty or so in the first chapter of St. Luke. The ubiquitous *waw* leaves its trail, not only of monotony but of obscurity. 'And thinking that he was in the company, they came a day's journey and sought him among their kinsfolk'—no; that is wrong; translate 'they had come a day's journey before they looked (really, before it occurred to them to look) for him among their kinsfolk'. 'Thinkest thou that I cannot ask my Father, and he will give me . . .'—no, that is wrong; anybody can *ask* for anything; translate, 'Thinkest thou that my Father will not give me, if I ask him . . .' And so on. Has the translator a right to recondition the whole system of sentence-coupling in the Bible? What makes the matter more urgent is that the conjunction in English is tending to die out, and we are concerned to budget for two hundred years hence. We say, 'I must find my coat, I've left my handkerchief in it', omitting the 'for'. We say, 'Don't touch that wire, or you will get a shock', not 'lest you should get a shock'. We never say, 'I didn't ask for lamb, but ham'; we say, 'I asked for ham not lamb', or, 'I didn't ask for lamb, I asked for ham'. Consequently, sentences like, 'Surely thou art one of them. For even thy speech doth discover thee', or 'Cast not your pearls before swine, lest they turn again', or 'I have not come to bring peace, but a sword' are out of date, and will come to wear more and more of an antique look as the years go by.

And, talking of that, what is the translator to regard as pure English? Is 'to abide in a place' over-antique; is 'to stay in a place' over-modern? And so on. It is not till you sit down to translate the Bible that words begin to haunt you with the sense of their evasiveness, and their caducity. *Mortalia facta peribunt, nedum sermonum stet honos et gratia vivax.* Here is a salient instance. For centuries people have laughed at the old Douay version, because in Galatians v. 4 it gave the rendering, 'You are evacuated from Christ'. In 1940, what metaphor could be more familiar, or more significant?

# III

# JUSTICE AND SCANDAL IN THE GOSPELS

In my essay on 'Some Problems of Bible Translation', I used the words: 'Under the Old Dispensation the *justus* is a man who is right with God, because he is careful to keep the law, moral and ceremonial; under the New Dispensation he is simply a justified person. . . . Or take the word *scandal*. . . . In the New Testament it means anything which *puts you off*, creates misgivings in you about the religious creed which you follow, or tends to do so'. I felt that these statements of mine were rather controversial, and half hoped they would produce some angry protest, to which I could make a full reply. It did not come, and I could not be at the trouble of writing a bogus protest myself. It seems more straightforward to publish, unsolicited, the answer which I should have made, if there had been any protest.

'In the prevailing use of the word by St. Paul, however, righteousness means the state of acceptance with God into which one enters by faith'. So writes Dr. Stevens in Hastings' *Dictionary of the Bible*, and it seems to me admirably put. He goes on to point out that when St. Paul talks about the righteousness (or justice) of God he means, predominantly, not that justice which is an attribute of God but the justice which God confers upon men; imputes to them if you will, imparts to them if you will, but something which resides in them, not in him. 'The justice of God is made manifest . . . even the justice of God, by faith of Jesus Christ, unto all and upon all

them who believe in him'—you do not begin to understand that sentence until you realize that it refers to *a*
justice (there is no article) *implanted by God* in the soul
of the believer; that is to say, a state of acceptance with
himself. To the Jew, justice was a state of the soul arising
out of, and manifested in, a faithful observance of the
law, moral and ceremonial. To the Christian, justice is a
state of the soul arising out of baptism, and the act of
faith which he makes in baptism. That is the contrast
which is familiar to us in St. Paul's writings. Are we to
assume that St. Paul invented this terminology (or simply
took it over from Hebrew thought), or has it any
parentage in the Gospels?

Here Dr. Stevens seems to me less helpful. *Dikaiosune*
in the Gospels, he writes, 'is not thought of under the
form of a status or relation; it is used rather in the simple
ethical sense, to include the qualities of a character which
is acceptable with God'. In the Gospels, according to his
view, the term has the same content, but with a different
emphasis. I wonder whether he has not reached this result
by concentrating too much on the fifth chapter of St.
Matthew? It is worth while trying to present, in bird's-
eye view, the whole catena of passages in the Synoptists
(St. John hardly matters), in which the words *justus* and
*justitia* occur.

Where pagans are speaking, Pilate or his wife or the
centurion, a just man is simply an innocent man (Matt.
xxvii. 19, 24; Luke xxiii. 47). The spies in Luke xx. 20
presumably feigned themselves to be honest men. Con-
ceivably, the justice of St. Joseph is emphasized in
Matthew i. 19 to explain why he wanted to put our Lady
away, or why he hesitated to put her away. These are the
only cases in which the word 'just' can be given its
modern, specialized sense. But there are two other

passages in which a just man appears to mean simply a
good man; where Herod recognizes that St. John the
Baptist is a just and holy man, and where God sends his
rain on the just and the unjust (Mark vi. 20; Matt. v. 45).

In other contexts, it is not clear whether the people
called just are so called simply because they possessed
desirable moral qualities, or because, possessing those
qualities, they enjoyed the status of being acceptable with
God. In three passages (Matt. x. 41, xiii. 17, xxiii. 29)
just men are bracketed with 'prophets', as if to imply a
somewhat lower degree of sanctity. Zachary and his wife,
Simeon, and Joseph of Arimathea are called 'just'; in the
first of these cases a legal touch is added to the descrip-
tion, when we are told that they 'were both just before
God, walking in all the commandments and justifications
of the Lord without blame' (Luke i. 6, ii. 25, xxiii. 50).
The Pharisees are anxious to appear just before men; but
they will be held responsible for the blood of all the just
men who have been killed, from the just Abel down to
Zacharias (Matt. xxiii. 28, 35). 'Acceptable with God'
would serve, in all these cases, as a possible synonym,
but it is not clear that the context demands it; 'upright'
would almost meet the situation.

In other passages again, the predominant sense of the
word *just* is surely one of status; the just are the people
of whom God approves, as contrasted with the people of
whom he disapproves. When we hear that at the last day
the just will shine out in their Father's kingdom (as if
they had been hitherto indistinguishable), that the angels
will separate, then and not before, the just from the
unjust (Matt. xiii. 43, 49), that the just will go into everlasting life, the wicked into everlasting fire (Matt. xxv.
46), it is surely a status (though here of justification plus
sanctification) which is implied. To be sure, the just have

earned their title by good works (Matt. xxv. 37), but un-
consciously. The 'resurrection of the just' (Luke xiv.
14) belongs to the same set of contexts. What can 'the
wisdom of the just' mean, unless it mean the wisdom
which justifies (Luke i. 16)? And our Lord has come to
call sinners, not the just (Matt. ix. 13 and parallels), in
the sense that the 'just' do not invite interference,
because they are, or think they are, already on the right
road; they need, or think they need, no repentance to put
them straight (Luke xv. 7). In the last two passages, it
looks as if our Lord was specially referring to people who
regard themselves as justified by the works of the law; as
he does explicitly in Luke xviii. 9, 'those who trust in
themselves, that they are just', whereas in fact the im-
moral publican is justified rather than the moral Pharisee.

I should claim, then, that if we were asked of some
passage in the Gospels, 'What does it mean by *just*?' it
would nearly always be possible to give 'acceptable to
God' or 'approved of by God' as a synonym, and as often
as not you would find it difficult to devise any other
synonym. What, then, of the noun, *justice*? I do not find
that it occurs above eight times in the Synoptists; but in
three of the eight passages it presents a cardinal difficulty
of translation.

The justice of Christians, which is to abound above
that of the Pharisees, is evidently a morality. And when
we are told not to 'perform our justice' before men, it
consists of a series of salutary acts, such as the Old Law
delighted to recognize (Matt. v. 20, vi. 1). To walk 'in
holiness and justice' before God (Luke i. 75) may also be
claimed as an instance where justice means the same
thing as uprightness, though here, as in Luke i. 6, it is
justice *before God*; the notion of claiming his approval is
not far absent. The Beatitudes curiously cancel out; if it

is more natural to think of pious souls as hungering and thirsting after God's approval, it is equally more natural to think of them as being persecuted for the sake of a moral principle (Matt. v. 6, 10). What are we to say, then, of the three remaining contexts: 'So it becometh us to fulfil all justice' (Matt. iii. 15), 'Seek ye therefore first the kingdom of God and his justice' (Matt. vi. 33), and 'John came to you in the way of justice, and you did not believe in him' (Matt. xxi. 32)?

I cannot understand how anybody remains content with 'justice' or 'righteousness' as a translation in the first of these passages. Justice is a thing you practise, not a thing you fulfil; and even if you substitute the word 'duty' you have not explained how or why it was a *duty* to be baptized by St. John. No law prescribed it, no prophet enjoined it. Surely the meaning sticks out of the passage, if you will only get away for a moment from the tyranny of words. To receive John's baptism is to make an effort—the best then available—to put yourself right with God. It was fitting that our Lord should receive this baptism for the same reasons—whatever they were—which made it fitting that he should undergo circumcision, another 'justifying' ceremony. 'It is fitting that we should win God's acceptance in every way we can'—that is not a translation, perhaps, but it surely gives the sense of the speech.

In the second passage, it is barely possible to interpret 'his justice' as meaning 'justice like his' (cf. Matt. v. 48). But such a rendering lacks both precedent and plausibility. This the old Douay translators evidently felt; they realized that a reference to God's *subjective* attributes was out of place, and gave us, not 'his justice', but 'the justice of him'. They evidently intended to bring this phrase into line with those alluded to above, where St.

Paul speaks of the justice of God; meaning thereby, not
the justice which God possesses, but the justice of which
he is author—that is, the state of justification. 'Seek ye
first the kingdom of God and his acceptance, his approval'; that is, surely, the obvious sense. At the beginning of the chapter, our Lord has warned us that we
should not aim at being justified in the sight of men; at
the end of it, he puts before us as of paramount importance the aim of being justified in the sight of God.

'John shewed you the way to be good'; so Dr.
Moffatt for *venit in via justitiae*—can any parallel be ad-
duced, any probability be urged, for this appallingly flat
rendering? The context, of course, with its reference to
the publicans and harlots believing, might lend a smudgy
colour to this sort of language. But Lagrange warns us not
to be led astray by the context: '*Venir dans une voie de
justice* est une locution sémitique pour indiquer une ex-
trême sollicitude à observer la loi . . . Jean est venu, et
precisément vers vous, et dans la voie de la justice qui
est votre fort'. It is a repetition of 'John came neither
eating nor drinking'; the strict Nazirite paradoxically
appeals to the lesser breeds without the Law, fails to
appeal to the Law's jealous custodians. John came with
all the strict observance which could be supposed, under
the Old Dispensation, to win God's acceptance; it was
all wasted on you.

In all these three passages, if nowhere else, I should
claim that the Pauline sense of *dikaiosune*, as the sum of
the conditions which qualify a soul for God's approval, is
the only key which fits the lock of the original without
groaning reluctance.

*Skandalon* is a word which has less of pre-history, less
of background, to confuse us. In the Old Testament it is

used, nearly always by a metaphor, in conjunction with *pagis*, a snare, or *lithos proskommatos*, a stumbling-block; and with the latter word it appears to be, by usage, convertible. It was first used (in the form *skandalethron*) of the spring which releases a trap and makes it suddenly shut on you. And I believe this element of *surprise* is nearly always, if not always, associated with it; a fact which commentators are apt to forget. To be scandalized is, primarily, to tread on a rake. Something gets up and hits you unexpectedly.

The word 'snare' would do for an interpretation of it, though not perhaps for a translation of it, in some of its most familiar contexts. 'If thy hand or thy foot is a snare to thee', that is, an occasion of falling (unexpectedly) into sin, gives you a fair idea of the meaning (Matt. v. 29, xviii. 8 and parallels). 'The angels will remove from his kingdom all the snares', all the evil examples that trapped us into sin—you do not need much more in the way of interpretation there (Matt. xiii. 41). Perhaps also 'Whoever lays a snare for one of these little ones. . . . Woe to the world because of such snares. . . . It must needs be that such snares should come', that is, bad examples which lead simple minds to contract evil habits before they realize that they are evil; that, too, is intelligible.

So much for the *scandalum pusillorum*; when we come on to the *scandalum Pharisaeorum*, it is not such plain sailing. A saying of our Lord's scandalizes the Pharisees (Matt. xv. 12), and St. Peter is directed to pay the didrachma 'so that we may not scandalize them' (Matt. xvii. 27). 'This saying laid a snare for the Pharisees', 'that we may not lay a snare for them'—it will not do; we must get closer to the root of the idiom. What was the trouble with the Pharisees? Not that they were shocked, exactly—that is a modern connotation of the term; not that they were indignant—that is a false inference from the Authorized Version's 'offended'. To be scandalized is, rather, to be 'put off'; if only slang were not so much more expressive than English! In a slang Bible, 'put off' would translate at least ninety per cent of the *scandalum* passages. You have been going along, so far, quite happy and undisturbed in your religious beliefs, your spiritual loyalties, and then *suddenly* something crops up, something seen or heard, which throws you out of your course; you have the feelings of a man who has tripped over some unseen obstacle and stumbled off the pathway into rough ground; *that* is to be scandalized.

If you are a *pusillus*, a humble disciple of Christ, and unexpectedly make some disedifying discovery about the Christian religion, then you are genuinely scandalized; you do not necessarily fall away, but you totter, for the moment, in your allegiance. If you are a Pharisee, broad-mindedly pretending that you have half a mind to become a disciple of Christ if all goes well, then the same disedifying discovery will scandalize you, but not genuinely. You pretend to feel disappointment, but as a matter of fact you find yourself rather relieved; no need to become a disciple now! You are finished with it, from now on! The official attitude of the Pharisees, at least in the earlier stages of our Lord's ministry, was one of taking an enlightened interest in our Lord's teaching; they were always asking questions, always offering to be convinced by a sign; sometimes, one would actually hold out hopes of conversion (e.g. Matt. viii. 19). But they did not really want to be convinced; when our Lord criticized their custom of hand-washing, it was a welcome excuse for saying, 'Well, that finishes it!' to hear that he did not pay the didrachma would have been an excuse even more unassailable. But always, observe, the thing that scandalizes must be an unexpected discovery; 'If I'd known *this*', you say, 'I would never have bothered to look into the thing'.

It is the same with the people of Nazareth, when they are scandalized by seeing our Lord in the synagogue there (Matt. xiii. 57 and parallel). The point is, surely, that they had heard of a great preacher, actually a Nazareth man, who had made a name for himself at Capharnaum and elsewhere, and flocked to the synagogue on the occasion of his visit. Only when he rose to speak did they discover, unexpectedly, that this was the boy who used to run errands from the carpenter's shop; what a disappointment! They had really hoped to listen to something worth hearing; but . . . the carpenter's son! Evidently these stories of effective preaching, of miraculous powers, must have been grossly exaggerated. It was the surprise of discovering our Lord's identity which suddenly tripped up their calculation, suddenly put them off, and determined them not to take any notice of what he said. They had come prepared to be impressed, but the unexpected revelation of his identity was too much for them.

From a different angle, the synagogue congregation at Capharnaum was scandalized by our Lord's first preaching of Eucharistic doctrine (John vi. 61). Here, the unexpected element in the situation which threw them off their balance would seem to be the sudden excursus into mysticism, on the part of a Teacher to whom they had looked, hitherto, for simple moral exhortation. It is difficult to label this *scandalum Pharisaeorum*; we have no reason to think that the followers who walked no more with our Lord after this had been, till then, insincere followers. Nor yet can we accuse our Lord of having given them that *scandalum pusillorum* against which his

most terrible warnings were uttered. In New Testament
usage, there is a kind of scandal which does not fall into
either of the theological categories. 'Ye did run well;
who hath hindered you?' (Gal. v. 7); it is possible to be
a genuine disciple, and yet to be thrown off your balance
by a scandal which came into the world through no
human fault.

This brings us on to a fresh set of passages in which
scandal is identified with persecution. Once more, let us
remind ourselves that persecution scandalizes *because it is
unexpected*. The sudden glare of the risen sun withers the
ill-rooted stalks of wheat all in a moment; so the ill-
rooted Christian is taken off his guard by the sudden in-
cidence of persecution (Matt. xiii. 21). He will be taken
off his guard like that, when he finds that to be a Christian
is to be hated of all men (Matt. xxiv. 10); 'Oh, come',
he will say, 'I never bargained for this; I never realized I
was letting myself in for this!' He is thrown off his
balance, by a scandal which is half Pharisaical; is he not
secretly relieved to have an excuse for deserting the nar-
row way? Most of us have known converts who were
scandalized like that, when they found that being a
Catholic was not making an easy choice, and fell away,
almost welcoming the opportunity. . . .

So it was, for a moment, with the apostles themselves.
Our Lord did everything to prevent the news of his
arrest coming as a sudden shock to them; just as he did
his best to prevent later persecutions coming as a sudden
shock to them, 'These things I have said to you that you
may not be scandalized', may not be taken off your guard
(John xvi. 1). But in fact the surprise will be too much
for them; 'all of you will be scandalized because of me
this night' (Matt. xxvi. 31), yes, even Peter will be
scandalized (Matt. xxvi. 33). For all their protestations,

when the crucial moment comes they will be found saying, 'We never bargained for this'.

It would appear to be in this sense that our Lord says,
in Matt. xi. 6, 'Blessed is he who is not scandalized in
me'. At first sight, 'scandalized in me' seems to suggest
that our Lord himself is a stumbling-block, that his
mission is itself something which 'puts people off'. But it
is hard to see how any sense can be made of such a rendering. It must mean, 'Blessed is he who, in his following
of me, is not put off by' something or other. By what?
Once more, I think, by persecution. St. John the Baptist
has consistently acclaimed our Lord as the Messias who
is to come; now he is tempted to doubt his own identi-
fication; what is the new factor, the unexpected factor in
the situation which has impressed him? His own im-
prisonment, I think; the continued triumph of evil over
good, unreversed by any Messianic *dénouement*. There will
often be times when the hour of deliverance seems to
have struck, and yet is delayed; blessed is he who, at such
times, is not put off by the apparent defeat of God's
cause.

One Gospel passage remains, in which the word *scandalum* occurs. 'Get thee hence, thou Satan, thou art a
scandal to me' (Matt. xvi. 23)—are we still moving in
the same ambit of thought? It has been suggested that
*skandalon* here means an obstacle; 'Thou art a hindrance
to me', Moffatt translates, as if St. Peter were barring our
Lord's path to Jerusalem. But where did *skandalon* ever
mean anything of the kind? It is not the barrier which
visibly bars your way; it is the loose stone or the trap
that catches your foot. Perhaps a stone is meant, in vivid
contrast to the *super hanc petram* of a moment ago; but
only a small stone, interrupting the evenness of the path.
Our Lord seems here, by condescension, to represent

D

himself as a *pusillus*, capable of being scandalized, of being thrown out of his true course by the bad advice offered him. 'You surprise me' would almost be a rendering; what more unexpected snare for those feet, Jerusalem-bound, than one laid by Peter? Though possibly, here, there is some hint of the language which treats human affection as a snare; so King Saul let Michal marry David, that she might be a snare to him (I Kings xviii. 21).

How to render *skandalizein* is a problem, even if you think you have got a consistent account of its meaning. Where *scandalum pusillorum* is concerned, 'to be an occasion of sin to' is literal, but perhaps in some places over-definite; 'to hurt the conscience of' is really nearer the mark. And perhaps, ironically, the latter rendering might do also for *scandalum Pharisaeorum*. In most of the other passages discussed above, I feel the nearest equivalent is 'to disappoint'; no other translation suggests that idea of unexpectedness which so dominates the metaphor.

# IV

# CHALLONER AND THE DOUAY VERSION[1]

FATHER Francis Blyth, sometime Vicar Provincial of the English Carmelites, is a figure little remembered. Yet, unobtrusively enough, he has left his mark on English-speaking Catholicism; it was he who collaborated with Bishop Challoner first in the editing, then in the re-writing, of the old Douay Bible. Like Challoner himself, he was one of the rare converts of that age; so that our present version of the Scriptures is altogether the work of men who had received the cadences of the Authorized Version with the ears of childhood. One may add, it was the work of men who instinctively thought of the Bible as a book meant to be read, not as a flinty deposit for theologians to quarry texts from. 'Two men wrote a Lexicon, Liddell and Scott; one half was clever, and one half was not'—it is always impossible to determine how much we owe to which collaborator, when a recension appears under such auspices. Our instinct is to guess that the less famous and the less busy of the pair did, at least, the greater part of the donkey-work. But it is to be presumed in any case that the Vicar Apostolic, not the Vicar Provincial, had the final say when it came to re-vision. Challoner must be the chief target for whatever praise or blame we are inclined to bestow on the undertaking.

And indeed the whole conception bears Challoner's

[1]An essay contributed to *Richard Challoner*, 1691–1781 (West-minster, 1946).

stamp. It was the age of the Encyclopædists; chill blasts of rationalism threatened to stunt the development of spirituality. And Challoner, like his contemporary John Wesley, saw that if a religious minority was to survive, it must have a culture of its own, a literature of its own. Like Wesley, he settled down with incredible energy to supply the lack himself, and formed, by sheer application, the type of culture which is still, on the whole, that of English Catholics, only leaving Faber to write the hymns. If we have since re-edited (for example) the *Garden of the Soul*, Challoner was the last man who would, or should, have complained. He was himself, like Wesley, an adapter, an abridger, a continuator, rather than an original genius. In an age when nobody wrote badly, he was content, like Wesley, to write a great deal moderately, never giving himself time to write anything really well. We must have stock meditations for every day in the year, we must have the lives of the martyrs re-written to a formula, we must have the Jesus Psalter purged of its old-world expressions, we must have our prayers stereotyped by a manual of devotions. The distant prospect of Emancipation was already in view; the tone, then, of English Catholicism must be English, must be cautious. There was to be no exuberance.

With such conditions imposed on him by the circumstances of his time, it is unlikely that Challoner ever considered the possibility of translating the Bible afresh. It was not an impossibility in that age; witness the version which gave, in James ii. 3, 'And he says to the fine suit of clothes, Sit you here; that's for quality'. A rendering like that might have done something to make even the eighteenth century think; for Challoner, the soporific effect of 'to him that is clothed with the goodly apparel' would do well enough, once you had changed 'goodly' into 'fine'. His instinct was all for darning and patching, for scratching out a word here and writing a new word over the top, never for re-conditioning. Moreover, there was an excellent source of inspiration ready to hand. In an age when Wesley was trampling on Young's copyright, and pirating Johnson's *Taxation no Tyranny* without acknowledgement, who would blame you for stealing your material, wherever possible, from the Authorized Version? After all, it was only occult compensation for the equally unacknowledged use of Douay in 1611.

What verdict we pass on Challoner's work—or Blyth's—must depend on the view we take of the Old Douay, which most English Catholics have never seen. Was it a priceless heritage which the eighteenth-century revisers ruined for us, or an indifferent compilation of which they made the best they could? And were the changes they made really substantial enough to alter its character? The answer to these questions is given in curiously different forms. Now you will be told that the old Douay was 'a version in cumbersome English, so full of Latinisms as to be in places hardly readable, but withal scholarly and accurate'; now that Challoner and Blyth 'sacrificed the energetic language of the older translators for a much weaker one which frequently lacks dignity'. Now you will find Challoner's work described as if it were merely a revised edition, now you will be told by Newman that the changes 'almost amount to a new translation', and by Wiseman that 'to call it any longer the Douay or Rhemish version is an abuse of terms'. The fact is, I think, that all these estimates are exaggerated.

I know it is the fashion to talk as if the old Douay was a really good translation. I am less moved by the fashion, than by the fact that John Phillimore used to say the same thing, and he knew what style was. But I think he was really in love with the *vocabulary* of Douay, its mere choice of terms. Here the charge of Latinism has been very much overdone. Everybody knows that in the second chapter of Philippians our Lord is said to have exinanited himself, and to have become an object of adoration to the 'celestials, terrestrials and infernals'. But it would be ridiculous to suppose that Gregory Martin often wrote in that way; his instinct was for sound Anglo-Saxon words, and only a verse or two lower down Challoner has had to alter 'murmurings and staggerings' into 'murmurings and hesitations'. The word 'wench', in spite of its pejorative associations, was seized upon by Gregory Martin as the right equivalent for *korasion* at the end of Mark v; and if you have the courage to use it, it is much better than the pretty-pretty word 'damsel', which Challoner borrowed (though it was obsolete by his time) from the Authorized Version. Phillimore's point was, I think, that the Authorized Version had impoverished our language by reducing its vocabulary to a small collection of stock words, which is certainly true. It uses the word 'destroy' to render about forty different verbs in the Hebrew.

But if you admire the *style* of the Douay, its syntax, its arrangement of the words in the sentence, what you are admiring is an accidental quaintness which Gregory Martin allowed himself, not because he thought it good prose, but because he felt bound to give a word-for-word translation, literal as Kelly's Keys, of everything that was in the Latin and nothing more. He did this on principle. He held that if you 'supplied' so much as an auxiliary verb, in order to make grammar of a sentence, you were *interpreting*; and that gave the heretics an excuse for interpreting the Bible in their own sense. The Authorized

Version, in Hebrews xiii. 4, gives you 'marriage *is* honourable in all'; it was an attack, Martin held, on celibacy, and it was bad scholarship. And, sure enough, the Revised Version and all the modern Protestant editions give you 'Let marriage be held in honour' or words to that effect. Not so Gregory; he would not interpret, for fear of giving the Protestants licence to interpret. His sentence runs, 'Marriage honourable in all and the bed undefiled', without any pretence of a main verb; grammar be hanged! So with the much better known passage in John ii; he wrote 'What is to me and thee woman?' and boasted in a footnote of having left the reader 'choice and indifferency' to interpret the meaningless phrase as he would. What was Challoner, with his neat eighteenth-century mind, to make of all this?

It is perhaps the greatest weakness of his version, that he is inconsistent; but you must not throw stones about inconsistency till you have tried making a version of the Bible yourself. In Hebrews xiii the ungrammatical sentence remains to this day. In John ii, he inserted the word 'that' after the word 'is', and thus fixed upon generations of English Catholics a false interpretation of the passage. (In passages like II Paralipomenon xxv. 31 not only Challoner, but Douay before him, had given the same idiom its right force, 'What have I to do with thee?') For the quaintnesses of the Douay, Challoner cared nothing; in an age when theologians were still chopping texts, there was better ground for respecting its pedantries. He would not admit 'righteousness' into his version; still clung to 'do penance' as a rendering of *pœnitentiam agere* (the Vulgate's effort to provide a personal verb meaning 'to repent'). In his time, as in the old days at Douay, Calvinism, not Pelagianism, was the enemy.

How much ought we to admire quaintness? It will always have the applause of the literary cliques. 'There was confusion of great death in the city' sounds well, means nothing. 'There was the confusion of a great mortality in the city' is flat by contrast; but can we really quarrel with Challoner for giving us an intelligible sentence? On the whole, we shall be inclined to blame him for falling between two stools. If he was going to make, on Newman and his contemporaries, the impression of having written a new version altogether, why did he not take his courage in both hands and write one? He will correct the old Douay where it is too literal to have any meaning at all; 'a vineyard was made to my beloved in horn, the son of oil' becomes 'my beloved had a vineyard on a hill in a fruitful place', and 'they have spoken in heart and heart' becomes 'with a double heart have they spoken'. If these Hebraisms were to be taken out of tangle, was it still necessary that King David's reins should be burned, or a right spirit introduced into his bowels? But I have every sympathy with the holy bishop in his hesitations—what Gregory Martin would have called his staggerings. I would give much to have some record of the private conferences that must have passed, perhaps in the suite of the Portuguese ambassador, between Challoner and Blyth. Was it Blyth, or was it Challoner himself, that first raised the question, how much the public would stand?

Meanwhile, what really grips the reader of the old Douay and makes him read on is not the text but the notes. These were not the work of Gregory Martin, but of Allen himself and a few others. Their length is prodigious, and they are consistently racy, as is all the controversial literature of that period. 'Singing psalms . . . one in this language and one in that, all together like a

Black Sanctus, and one often not understood of another'—what more engaging picture could you have of the early Corinthian church? But the notes contained a good deal of explosive material, not by any means suited to an age in which Emancipation had begun to be imaginable. The Irish bishops found that out to their cost, early in the next century. 'Simon Magus more religious than the Protestants' made a good headline, but it was not calculated to endear Catholics to their fellow countrymen. The notes were ruthlessly cut out; occasionally you will meet the ghost of one, in the Old Testament especially (the one about the mystical significance of Tobias's dog, for instance), but the glory has departed.

It is well to remember that the Douay, whether in its Martin or in its Challoner state, has suffered from unfair competition. England has long possessed a standardized version of the Bible, whose hieratic phrases, familiar in days when there was more religion about, have seeped into every runnel of our language. Droned into the ears of youth for a matter of four centuries, its cadences have come to be accepted as the right sort of cadences, and are what the ordinary Englishman means by good prose. Whether the effect of Bibliolatry on English style has really been a gain, Phillimore doubted, and Mr. Somerset Maugham has doubted more recently. Certainly it has impoverished our vocabulary; or why is Shakespeare such a mass of obsolete words? But in a country with a totalitarian prose tradition, any rendering of a Bible phrase which is not looted bodily from the Authorized Version sounds like bad prose. And Challoner's borrowed plumes only set off the discrepancy; in bulk, the Douay sounds to a Protestant ear barbarous and exotic. But that is because the other lot won.

Did Challoner hope that his revised Bible would come to be known and loved by English Catholics, as the Authorized Version was known and loved by their neighbours? It was perhaps not too late; in the eighteenth century, readers were already numerous, and books still few. But whether from inherited distrust, or because after all his efforts the Bible remained mostly unintelligible, the result never followed. To this day, so far as English-speaking Catholics are concerned, the Bible consists of a handful of fragments read out in Church, two psalms, a remembered phrase here and there in the liturgy, and a few dozen dogmatic texts.

## V

## SOME REASONS WHY

THERE is no saving this essay from a certain air of exhibitionism. I may reasonably be asked whether it is not enough to foist off a new version of Scripture on the public, without proceeding to explain to them why they ought to like it. But I do not see how else I am to express my gratitude to many who have had faults to find with my translation, and written to tell me so—still less, how to express it to those who had faults to find and did not write to tell me so. A criticism can usually be set out in a few lines; the reply to it demands, commonly, ten times the space. And when people have written to me making suggestions—usually suggestions which had already been made, and set aside—I have for the most part contented myself with saying that I had made a mark against the passage and would think it over; I simply had not the paper, let alone the time, to explain my reasons to each. What I propose to do here is to reprint, with a friend's permission, some criticisms which occurred to him or to his friends, in his own words; then to make my defence as best I can. I think he differs from most of my correspondents in that he genuinely wants me to convince him, instead of wanting to convince me. But he is not a mere man of straw, put up by me to attack my efforts at translation, just where I think the opportunity of defence is strongest. His are genuine criticisms; those of a man well versed in the classics and in English literature, and with a mind of great exactitude. Since he does not wish me to mention his name, we will christen him Glaucon.

49

His main complaint is that I am too periphrastic. It is a vice which besets the translator; you interpret your original, necessarily, in a series of mental periphrases, and these must be reduced to plain language again when you put pen to paper—it is like coding and decoding. Glaucon is doubtful whether I have managed the second part of the process. He writes:

'Your Epistles are bejewelled with excellent verbs; why are you so periphrastic elsewhere? From St. Matthew one might quote "offer resistance to" (v. 39), "it is my will" (viii. 3), "has brought thee healing" (ix. 22), "make room for it in your minds" (xi. 14), "made answer to" (xii. 48), "gave her no word in answer" (xv. 23)—each representing a single Greek verb. But there are two outstanding examples. Surely "it is within your knowledge how . . ." (Acts xx. 18, xxii. 19; I Thess. ii. 11) is pure journalese? Are you going to make Job say, "It is within my knowledge that my Redeemer is alive"? And why "have sight of" (Matt. xvii. 3, xxviii. 7; John xvi. 16; Acts xxii. 14; Apoc. v. 3)? This strikes me, not as journalese, but as preciosity. True, the verb "see" *can* be used in very trivial contexts, and the sight of Moses and Elias was far from trivial. But you, like everyone else, write "they shall see God" in Matt. v. 8. If, then, "see" is adequate for the Beatific Vision, can there be any earthly vision whatsoever for which it is inadequate?'

I suppose we should all admit that English is a language of nouns, rather than of verbs. The New Oxford Dictionary will always give you your noun *first*, even with a word like 'lead', where the noun is only a derivative. Contrast this with Brown, Driver and Briggs' Hebrew Dictionary, where the verb (unless it is an obvious back-formation) always takes precedence of the noun; and if there is no verb of the kind to be found in extant Hebrew documents, Brown, Driver and Briggs invent it for you. It would be easy to preach a sermon on the subject; do we, perhaps, judge too much by results, whereas the language of the Angels concentrates its attention on the process by which the results are attained? But for my present purposes I only want to put on record (the French have a verb for it, *constater*) the fact that it is so. And it will hardly be denied that this tendency is a growing one. The modern reporter in the *Eatanswill Guardian* has long been in the habit of telling us that Mr. Stiggins 'was the recipient of' a gold watch from his admiring parishioners; and the other day I saw it in *The Times*. Worse is coming; the Basicists have decided to get on with a mere handful of verbs, and will tell us that 'Vasco da Gama was going in a ship round the sides of Africa', to avoid adding the word 'sail' to their vocabulary.

With the Basicists I am not concerned, except to point out that in so far as their movement comes to anything, it will probably react on normal English usage. For the journalist, I have more sympathy. It is not, I think, that he is simply out to use a long Latin word. He wants his sentence to have punch, and he sees that the good old verb 'give' has largely lost its punch, through over-use and over-wide application. You *give* Mr. Jones a gold watch; but you can also *give* him a clout on the ear, or a nod, or an account of what happened at the match yesterday, or a wide berth, or a start, or a hole at golf; and the result is that the word 'give' is tending to become bleached and discoloured. The point is not that it is often used in frivolous connexions. The point is that it is so widely used in all sorts of connexions as to lose its strength. It no longer hits the mind with a sense of *generosity*. But the word 'recipient', unpleasing as it is, does impress on the casual reader that somebody has been generous to somebody.

I am not concerned to defend Gigadibs; my point is that the journalese of one generation tends to become the normal prose of the next. And here I must make an admission which will earn me plenty of cold looks. The man who sits down to translate the Bible slips, as a rule, into the idiom of his grandfathers. He thinks his own contemporaries will be rather impressed at language two centuries out of date; he forgets that his own version, if it is accepted, will last two hundred years longer; by which time the die-hards will all be protesting against the blasphemy of altering a word of it, while the general public will be wondering what on earth it is all about. My own idea has been to secure, as far as possible, that Englishmen of 2150, if my version is still obtainable then, shall not find it hopelessly 'dated'. While, therefore, I am not going to use journalese, if I can help it, I am not going to neglect those tendencies in the development of the language (partly encouraged by journalism) which you can see to be constant. For example, the co-ordinating conjunctions, 'for', 'but', even 'and', grow rarer in common English speech, and they are rare in my version. Similarly, I have allowed myself to use nouns instead of verbs, where I think the noun makes a neater impress on the mind, of the casual reader especially—and how many readers, in these days, are not casual?

'Herod will search for the child' suggests to my mind Herod poking about in the shrubbery; when he sends pursuivants out to kill all the children in and around Bethlehem I call it 'making search for the child'—the process is an elaborate one, best represented by an elaborate phrase. 'Thou hast power to make me clean' gives room for an emphasis of which the word 'canst' is incapable; if you let your voice dwell on the word 'canst' you immediately find yourself implying 'but of course I know you're not going to'. Again, for some reason you cannot say 'I pity the multitude' without suggesting contempt; 'I am moved with pity for the multitude' has no such unfortunate associations.

So with Glaucon's instances. For some reason we only use the verb 'resist' when the thing resisted is an imponderable—a tendency, or an influence, or something of that kind. When the allied troops entered a town you heard, not that nobody resisted them, but that nobody offered them any resistance. 'I will, be thou made clean' is, for modern ears, an *inaccurate* translation. Because instinctively you read 'I will' as a mere auxiliary verb, stating an intention; our Lord is saying something different, he is saying: 'You wonder whether I have the will to do this; well, as a matter of fact I have'. 'If you will make room for it in your minds'—surely 'if you will receive it' is meaningless to our ears? 'If you can take it,' we say; slang is always vigorous, but I try to resist the temptation of translating the Bible into slang. What else could one say? 'Made answer to' and 'gave her no word in answer' are, I admit, artificial phrases, but they bite, as the much over-used word 'answer' does not bite. 'Has brought thee healing' is perhaps in a different category. 'Has saved thee' surely implies too much of a theological event, 'has healed thee', too much of a merely medical event? *Salvam te fecit* (not, by the way, *salvavit*) is a supremely difficult turn of phrase to render.

In particular, I would defend the use of the words 'had sight of'. When a phrase dominates the decisive line of what is possibly the best sonnet in the language, you cannot dismiss it as a mere circumbendibus, the coinage of a pernickety translator.

'Have sight of Proteus rising from the sea,
    Or hear old Triton blow his wreathed horn'—

surely, even if the rhyme had been 'ocean' instead of 'sea', Wordsworth would have spoiled his line by writing:

'To see wise Proteus rising from the ocean'?

He wanted the actual privilege of witnessing, with eyes accustomed to drab Victorian sights, the invasion of our world by fairy people. So, I would urge, our Lord's disciples didn't merely 'see' Moses and Elias, as they might have 'seen' a rabbit scuttling down the rocks. They were privileged with a vision of the supernatural world. Hence, not *viderunt*, but *apparuerunt illis*; I hope no one will defend the hideous construction, 'there appeared to them', here as often used by the Authorized Version? Yet you *must* keep the content of the vision to the end of the sentence, so as to emphasize it. And when the Apostles went into Galilee after the Resurrection, it wasn't merely a casual encounter, like 'See you at the Old Boys' Dinner, I suppose?' When they reached Galilee, their eyes were to witness the truth of an inconceivably important fact; they were to gratify their passionate longing to look at the Face they knew. I don't see how you are to call the reader's attention (always ready to wander where the Bible is concerned) to the point of the story without slowing it up a bit, and saying 'There you shall have sight of'—something worth a million Proteuses.

Glaucon objects that, in order to be consistent, I should have written, 'Blessed are the pure in heart; they shall have sight of God'; he might also want me to have written, 'Sir, we would have sight of Jesus', in John xii. 21. But, apart from the fact that my committee were nagging at me a good deal for not leaving the Beatitudes as they stood (as being one of the New Testament passages Catholics are supposed to know by heart), I don't think I felt the need of periphrasis there. 'Seeing God' is from any merely natural point of view such a direct contradiction in terms that it arrests the mind (I think) without difficulty. Even as a matter of rhythm, the two stressed monosyllables, 'see' and 'God', warn the reader to go slow; he gets no such warning with 'they saw Moses and Elias', or 'there you shall see him'. As for the Greeks at the pasch, I have never been quite clear what the nature of their demand was; i.e. whether they were not merely asking to 'see' our Lord in the modern sense of 'having an interview with him', as presumably in Galatians i. 18. I don't think the context justifies you in making a splash of the thing.

I am much less certain about the circumlocution 'it is within your knowledge that'. I don't admit that it is journalese; it is rather, I should say, lawyer's English; it is the sort of thing the Chairman says to a committee, 'Gentlemen, it is within your knowledge'. I have used it on three occasions, rather as a *faute de mieux*. Certainly 'you know' will not do; nor 'they know' in Acts xxii. 19. This use of the verb 'to know' is essentially a Hebraism. In English, when we know that a man knows a thing we don't tell him that he knows it; we just state the fact. An English sentence beginning with the words 'you know' is either a question, leading on to a further statement (as, 'You know that pub at the end of Smith Street? It was burnt out last night'), or else a reproach involving a charge of inconsistency (as, 'You *know* you always tell me to turn the electric stove off when I leave

E

the drawing-room'). We are all fond of the phrase 'I know that my Redeemer liveth', partly because it is a favourite motet at Anglican funerals. But if you examine it in cold blood, as an English sentence, it obviously implies, 'I know that my Redeemer liveth, but I see no evidence that *I* shall'. It certainly won't be allowed to stand like that when I get to Job. In the last analysis, 'I know that my Redeemer liveth' is merely a Hebrew way of saying, 'My Redeemer liveth'.

The word 'know' is a constant problem to the translator, all through the New Testament. Nine times out of ten you want to translate it 'realize' but unfortunately that use of the word 'realize' is modern slang. In two of the cases Glaucon cites he has overlooked one point which makes the difficulty worse than ever. The Latin for 'you know' is *scitis*, and the Latin for 'they know' is *sciunt*. But it isn't *scitis*, it's *vos scitis*; and it isn't *sciunt*, it's *ipsi sciunt*. St. Luke, here, is not using Aramaic sources, and he must be credited with the intention of emphasizing his pronouns. In English there is no way of emphasizing a pronoun without the use of italics; and I am not going to use italics in my version. Therefore periphrasis is a necessity; you cannot translate your original without it; 'you know' is an *inaccurate* translation. What periphrasis can one use? 'Nobody knows better than you', 'You know if nobody else does', 'You at any rate know'—something of that kind? I confess that I would prefer one of these to the rather stilted form of speech I have used, but I know they would make people just as angry as it makes Glaucon. People *will* not see the difficulties, the real difficulties, of a translator. Arguably, the right rendering of St. Paul's speech to the elders is 'You yourselves can testify'[1]; it won't do in Thessalon-

[1] This change has since been made.

ians, because that phrase has occurred in the previous verse; in Acts xxii. 19, I am inclined to think 'it is within their knowledge' does really ring the bell.

A quite different principle is raised by Glaucon's next objection, although on the surface it looks as if it were part of the same grievance. He takes exception to my rendering of *credidit*, *crediderunt* (representing an aorist) in passages like John ii. 11, xx. 8, Acts iv. 4, xiii. 12. I should perhaps explain that there is a history behind the rendering in question ('learned to believe'). I had at first made a flat rule of translating 'found faith', which I still hold is the most accurate equivalent. This, however, evoked the liveliest protests from my committee, and with my usual weakness I tried to humour them. In most of the passages, not quite all, I consented to say that so-and-so 'learned to believe'. The concession afforded little pleasure to my committee, and to Glaucon none at all. He writes:

'Why do you boggle at "they believed" for *episteu-san*? True, the transition from one *external state* to another cannot be described by a simple aorist—"I lived at Puckeridge on April 1st" will not do for "I went to live at . . ."—but an aorist adequately describes the first entry into a continuing *mental condition*: "Dante loved Beatrice at first sight"; "the jury believed the evidence of Mrs. Bardell"; "I met Mrs. Snooks yesterday and admired her". If "admired" suffices for "became an admirer" why cannot "believed" suffice for "became a believer"? And even the "external" verbs have a true perfect. "Anyone who has lived at Puckeridge knows . . ." is good English. Why then must you write (John xx. 29), "Blessed are those who . . . have learned to believe"?

'But even if "believed" is unacceptable, is "learned

to believe" any improvement? We can learn *a fact* on
the 9 o'clock News, but learning *to do* is a process
which takes months or years. Many of us, as Pasteur
knew, go on "learning to believe" all our lives, but
*episteusan* is an act, not a process, and "learn", which
lays stress on the process, seems more than usually in-
appropriate in John xx. 8, which describes St. John's
instantaneous conviction that our Lord had risen.'

Glaucon, it will be seen, admits that you cannot use
the plain verb to express transition from one *external*
state to another; you must say that Queen Victoria 'began
to reign', not that she 'reigned', in 1837. But he draws a
distinction; you can, he suggests, use the plain verb
where you are describing the transition from one *internal*
state to another. Let us examine his instances.

The first of these is singularly revealing. It is not an instance of current English usage at all. It is a quotation
from Shakespeare, 'Who ever loved, that loved not at
first sight?' And it goes down, because you are talking
about Dante, who lived a long time ago. But give the
situation a modern setting, and the plausibility of his argument vanishes at once. Would he, or anyone else, tolerate
the phrase in a modern letter or novel, 'He met a girl at
Malta and loved her?' Does not the very existence of the
cumbrous periphrasis 'fall in love' bear witness to the fact
that 'loved', in such cases, represents an imperfect,
never an aorist?

'The jury believed the evidence of Mrs. Bardell' is
not, in fact, current English. We should say, 'The jury
were convinced by Mrs. Bardell's statements', or, more
colloquially, 'The jury took Mrs. Bardell's word for it'.
But, whether or no Glaucon's sentence is natural English,
it is not a true parallel. The New Testament gives you
situations in which a determining factor suddenly emerges

to turn unbelief into belief. But Mrs. Bardell's evidence was not a mere factor of this kind; it would be ridiculous to expect the jury to believe Mrs. Bardell's evidence *before they had heard it*. Nor does St. John say, 'Christ turned water into wine, and his disciples believed that he had turned water into wine'; he says, 'Christ turned water into wine, and thereupon his disciples passed into a general state of belief *in him*'. If the jury had at first been inclined to doubt Mrs. Bardell, and then Pickwick had suddenly gone white or fainted, we should be told, 'After this, the jury began to think there might be something in Mrs. Bardell's evidence', not 'The jury believed Mrs. Bardell's evidence'. And in any case they would only have believed in her veracity as a witness in that particular trial; no estimate of her general worth would necessarily be implied.

To say 'I met Mrs. Snooks yesterday and admired her' is not the same as saying 'I met Mrs. Snooks yesterday and became her admirer'. The former statement could only gratify Mr. Snooks; the latter might impel him to call me out. To 'become the admirer' of a woman implies crossing an important dividing line, just as to 'become a believer' does. If you simply say that you met her and admired her, you do not lay emphasis on a transition of feeling. Indeed, as it stands, the sentence implies that you met her yesterday for the first time; and how on earth were you to admire her when you had never met her? But you may 'become an admirer' of a woman you have known for years. Just so Chesterton, I think, in *The Napoleon of Notting Hill*, says you can see a thing for the thousandth time and suddenly, in doing so, see it for the first time. So it is when a man falls in love with a woman; so it is when a soul, which perhaps has been right up against the Church for years (as Chesterton was), suddenly gets the grace of faith. He does not simply 'believe'; he becomes a believer.

In the Acts, I think the true rendering of *credidit* is, 'he was baptized'; the late Professor of Divinity at Oxford introduced me to this consideration years ago, and I fully accept it. But I had not the courage to use the words in my translation; after all, the sacred authors allude, not to the ceremony of baptism, but to the act of faith which accompanies it. In St. John, the thing is much more complicated; he even seems to allow for two moments of adherence to Christ—one in which you come to believe in him as a true Prophet (if not more) as in John ii. 11, one in which you come to believe in him as having risen from the dead, as in John xx. 8. But in St. John, as in the Acts, what the author means to express is sudden emergence from a state of non-belief (or call it, if you like, prebelief), into what is, or ought to be, a lifelong state of believing.

I welcome Glaucon's point about the use of the perfect tense. Quite true, you can say, 'Anybody *who has loved* knows this or that'. But in saying that, you do not say that they stuck to it; if anything, you imply the contrary. When our Lord says, 'Blessed are those who have believed', does he include those who used to believe and have ceased to? Does he include Goebbels and Himmler? Very well then, the phrase 'have believed' gives you the wrong emphasis. At the back of their minds, the people who made the Authorized Version knew this. In John viii. 31, they translated the Greek perfect participle as if it were a present participle; they knew it would look silly to translate 'Then Jesus said to the Jews who had believed in him', so they left out the 'had'.

But, granted that you need two different formulas for expressing (*i*) the state of being a believer, and (*ii*) the process of coming into that state, is 'learn', asks Glaucon, the right word to use? He objects that learning is a thing which takes time, whereas my process of 'learning to believe' is a matter of a split second. I don't enormously like 'learning to believe'; but 'began to believe' is ambiguous, suggesting a half-way stage, and 'came to believe' would seldom be tolerable. I do not admit Glaucon's distinction between 'learning to' and 'learning that'. There is, it seems to me, an applied (almost a metaphorical) use of the verb, with which we are all familiar. Milton, who wrote:

'Henceforth I learn that to obey is best,'

also makes St. Michael promise to Adam a revelation of the future, which will enable him

'to learn
True patience, and to temper joy with fear.'

Learning is the correlative of teaching, and when a schoolmaster says, 'I'll teach you to throw stones at my window', the process indicated (though perhaps not as momentary as the pupil could wish) does not mean long weeks of laborious study. Surely it is good English to say that somebody 'learned to look both ways before crossing the street', as the result of a single accident?

Glaucon's next complaint deals with a quite different point; one, probably, which has exercised the reader more than those hitherto mentioned. In translating a sacred text, of which many older versions have become familiar, you are naturally pulled up now and again by the consideration, 'Will the public stand a rendering so different from the rendering it is accustomed to?' I do not profess to have dismissed this consideration altogether from my mind; and, once you allow it to weigh with you at all, you are easily betrayed into inconsistencies. It appears to Glaucon (or to his friends) that I have not avoided this pitfall. He writes:

'On what principle do you retain or reject archaisms? "Restored be thy health" is certainly not current English, nor does even patriotism induce us to say "Hail Churchill"; yet you do not alter a word of the Paternoster or the Angelic Salutation. Dramatic moments call for economy of phrasing, but you practise no economy when you write "Lazarus, come out here" (John xi. 43), "See, here is the man" xix. 5), "I am thirsty" (xix. 28). Surely here, if anywhere, the familiar archaisms are preferable to flaccidity?'

I need hardly say that 'Restored be thy health' is not a phrase I have used in my translation; it is only a parallel to illustrate the words 'Hallowed be thy name', which I have preserved in the Paternoster. My principle (if it can be called a principle) was to leave familiar prayer-forms untouched; but of these there are only two, the Pater and the Ave. (The Psalms, I am afraid, call for more radical treatment, and nothing will induce me to let king David pray for the renewing of a right spirit within his bowels.) In the story of the Passion I have introduced as much of the old version into my work as is consistent with Matthew ix. 16. But I could not see my way to adopting here (as I had to adopt in the prayer-forms) a definitely obsolete way of writing. I would have liked to write 'I thirst', but it would have stood out a mile from the context as a piece of Elizabethan English, and the effect would be, I think, painfully ugly. I had less scruple about *Ecce homo*, because I have never been able to see that 'Behold the man!' is a translation of it. The Latin for 'Behold the man!' is *Aspicite hominem*; to translate *Ecce homo* quite literally, you would have to print it with a comma, 'Behold, the man!' which is poor English of any period. What Pilate said, of course, was 'Here is the fellow'—*homo*, not *vir*. I have enough reverence for tradition to retain the word 'man', but not enough to retain a form of speech which does no justice to what Pilate was in fact saying. 'Lazarus, come out here' has been altered in the published edition, but not, I'm afraid, in a way which will give Glaucon any satisfaction, for the phrase becomes even longer, 'Come out, Lazarus, to my side'. 'Lazarus, come forth,' misses, surely, a point in the Greek (though the Latin has missed it too); the word *deuro* is an invitation, a beckoning, 'come *to me*'. But I confess that in any case my principles wouldn't have allowed me to use the word 'forth', which is, regrettably, obsolete.

I include one last criticism, more because it illustrates so well the difficulty of pleasing everybody, than for any importance of its own. One of Glaucon's friends had written complaining that I had turned the 'pale horse' of Apocalypse vi. 8, into a 'cream-white' horse. My objection to the word 'pale' is that it does not denote a colour; was it pale blue or pale pink or what? The whole heraldry of the chapter demands four different colours, white, red, black, and—what? It must be something distinguishable from pure white, and it seems to me an advantage if you can get a term which would be familiar at Tattersall's. A cream horse is sufficiently opposed to a white horse; and the Greek adjective is used by medical writers as the equivalent of 'yellow, bilious-looking'. At the same time, I said that I thought the adjective in question was probably used by the writer in its literal sense of 'green'. White, red, black and green—it was a vision, after all.

This sets Glaucon off again on his own:

'St. John tells us that he saw Death riding on a green horse—chloros, just like the "green things" in ix. 4. Why not take his word for it? You do not call the red horse a roan. In a world where locusts have women's hair and lions' teeth, where dragons have seven heads and ten horns, a green horse need cause no surprise. Green, for Death, seems exactly right; cream-white, a festal colour, exactly wrong.'

I don't think I agree with the last part; black would seem to me more appropriate than green as a symbol of death. Curiously, Coleridge makes death ride on a *white* horse:

'He saw an apothecary on a white horse
    Ride by on his own vocations,
And it put him in mind of his old friend,
    Death in the Revelations.'

I don't think my committee would have stood for a green horse. But my motive for avoiding it was a perfectly simple one—*I was translating the Vulgate.* I don't mind 'interpreting' the Vulgate to the extent of risking 'cream-white' when it gives you 'pale', which is not a colour. But when the Vulgate definitely avoids translating *chloros* 'green', and elects in favour of the wider meaning, I feel bound to follow it. I have done so in many places with regret; I have, for instance, given 'angel' in Matthew xi. 10. I know 'messenger' is right, but I cannot see how the American Revisers get 'messenger' out of the Latin *angelum*.

One man's meat is another man's poison; and I imagine that most people who have had the patience to read some of my New Testament version, and then to read this essay, will be angrily muttering that Glaucon has taken me up on the wrong points; *they* could have given me far worse teasers. I shall be very ready to defend myself against assault from other quarters. But at least I hope the length of this essay will have brought home to some of my brethren how difficult it is to answer one's critics in a short space.

# VI

# NINE YEARS' HARD [1]

I HAVE spent the last nine years, when not otherwise em-
ployed, in translating the Holy Bible from beginning to
end. I could have made rather better time, if it had not
been for the necessity of replying, sometimes in print
but far more often in private correspondence, to the
criticisms and the queries of the public. You see, it is no
ordinary task. If you translate, say, the *Summa* of St.
Thomas, you expect to be cross-examined by people
who understand philosophy and by people who understand Latin; no one else. If you translate the Bible, you
are liable to be cross-examined by anybody; because
everybody thinks he knows already what the Bible means.
And the form which these questions take is a very interesting one; nearly always it is, 'Why did you *alter* such
and such a passage?' Why did I *alter* it—when you say
you are going to translate the Bible, it is assumed that
you do not mean to do anything of the kind. It is assumed
that you mean to revise the existing translation, with
parts of which we are all familiar; altering a word here
and a word there, like a compositor correcting proofs
with a pair of tweezers. The more you plagiarize from the
work of previous interpreters, the better your public
will be pleased. In the few minutes now at my disposal, I
do not mean to answer, in general or in detail, that kind
of objection. I mean simply to discuss some of the difficulties which attend the process of *translating* the Bible;
really translating it, in the sense of approaching it as if
nobody had ever translated it before.

[1] A broadcast talk given on Radio Eireann.

In all translation, I suppose three things are expected of the interpreter. You must find out what the original means; you must try to express in your own language what the other man was trying to express in his. Nor can you do this by a merely literal rendering. If you are translating a French author, and come across the phrase, '*il se noya*', your first instinct is to translate it literally, 'he drowned himself'. But then you have to reflect that '*se noyer*' in French need not mean to drown oneself; it may mean simply to get drowned. Was it accident or suicide? You must find out from the context; if that is impossible, you must *hedge*; 'he met his death by drowning' will leave it doubtful whether it was suicide or not. Nor is it enough to find out what the man said, you must find out why he said it; you must reproduce, not only the sense, but the emphasis of his words. To take a very simple instance, which is constantly recurring, the Hebrew has one word that does duty for 'and' and 'but'; and wherever the translator comes across that word in the Old Testament he must decide between them, sometimes at the risk of making nonsense of a whole paragraph. And finally, if your original has any pretensions to literary merit, you want to preserve the rhetoric of it, which (commonly at least) you cannot do by a literal translation. '*Être ou ne pas être, c'est bien là la question*' is not Shakespeare.

There are special difficulties about finding out the exact meaning of any word in the New Testament. It was written, or at any rate it has come down to us, in Greek; and in a kind of Greek which had become debased through being used as the *lingua franca* of the civilized world, very much what Latin was in the Middle Ages. You can never be quite certain, therefore, how much of its native force a given word has preserved; just as you

cannot be certain whether the word *almus* in a Latin
hymn is meant to convey its root sense of 'nourishing', or
is a merely insipid epithet meaning 'kindly'. Worse than
that; most of the New Testament authors knew Greek
as a foreign language, and when you are talking a foreign
language you do not express your meaning exactly as a
native would. To take an extreme instance, an Irish-
man talking English does not use the words 'Yes' and
'No' like an Englishman; he says 'I did', or 'It is not',
because the language of his forefathers had no words for
'Yes' and 'No'. How are we to be certain, then, that
our author picked out the exact word to express what he
meant, writing as he was in a foreign medium? Take, for
example, St. Mark's account of our Lord's Agony in
Gethsemani. 'He began to fear and to be heavy'; so our
Bible translates it, but you will scarcely find two interpreters who are agreed on the proper rendering of either
verb. How much of fear, how much of astonishment, is
implied by the one; how much of hesitation, how much
of repining, by the other? And yet it is surely a matter of
importance that we should know exactly what our Lord
did feel in Gethsemani! Or take that well-known phrase
in the Last Gospel, 'the light shines in darkness, *et
tenebrae eam non comprehenderunt*'—does that mean that the
darkness could not understand it? Or that the darkness
could not smother it? Constantly you feel that the tool
which came to your author's hand was not the exact tool
he wanted.

But there is a further source of confusion. The New
Testament writings come down to us from a time when
the vocabulary of the Christian faith was in the making.
Words like grace, faith, salvation and so on, which have,
for us, an exact theological meaning, were being used
with less precision; they were not yet technical terms.

Consequently, the translator is always having to ask himself, 'Should this word in this particular passage be interpreted strictly, in its defined theological sense? Or is it still being used in a loose, popular way?' We translate 'Hail, thou that art full of grace', and in the next chapter 'Jesus grew in favour with God and man'; but the word 'grace' is the same as the word 'favour' in the original. We translate 'My faithful witness, Antipas'; but ought we, perhaps, to translate 'My faithful martyr'? By the time the Apocalypse was written, it may be that the term had already an official connotation. 'Sin'—that word was used by the Jews to designate any breach of the law, culpable or inculpable; and they were apt to describe their Gentile neighbours as 'sinners', meaning no more than that they were Gentiles. 'The Son of Man shall be handed over to sinners' means, almost certainly, 'The Son of Man shall be handed over to Gentile folk, the Romans'. When our Lord ate 'with publicans and sinners', were they people of notoriously evil life? Or were they merely Gentiles? 'Tend the church of God, in which the holy Spirit has made you bishops'—should it be 'bishops'? Or should it be just 'overseers'? Constantly the doubt recurs, 'Am I making the language of the New Testament too vague? Or am I making it too stereotyped? Am I reading too much into it, or too little?'

All this the translator must take into account if he is going to do justice to an individual phrase, an individual sentence. But his duty does not end there; he must follow the *thought* of his original, and make it intelligible to the reader, bringing out the emphatic word or words in each sentence, indicating its logical connexion with what goes before and what follows. He must make the whole paragraph hang together and convey a message. That duty was apt to be overlooked by the older translators, if only for this reason—that the Bible was printed in verses; and, by a trick of our natures, if a page of print is broken up to the eye, we do not expect it to convey any coherent impression to the mind. Any verse in the Bible was a 'text'; you preached from it, you quoted it in theological arguments, you did not look to see what the setting of it was, or how it fitted in. We are so accustomed to this piece-meal way of approaching the Bible that hundreds of priests, well enough grounded in Latin, read the epistle for Christmas Eve without noticing that there is no main verb in it.

I don't say that it is easy to bring out the general sense of a Biblical passage. Sometimes, for example, in the Prophets, you have to give up, and admit that these passages may have been intelligible to the people they were written for, but certainly aren't to us. But in St. Paul's epistles, for example, or in the Book of Job, it is quite clear that there is a thread of argument running all through, though it is very far indeed from lying on the surface. To present your material so that this thread of argument becomes apparent is no easy matter; but you have got to do it, if the Bible is to be read as a book, and not merely studied as a lesson.

I said it was the translator's business, in the third place, to preserve the idiom of his original. That means, not that he must copy it, which would be easy enough; he must transpose it into the idiom of his own language. Some of us, when we were at school and did Latin, studied that splendid outburst of Cicero against Catiline in the Roman senate, which begins, 'How long, O Catiline, will you abuse our patience?' At least, that was how we rendered it, and thereby ruined it; you lose all the force of the original. We should have said, 'What, Catiline! Still taking advantage of our forbearance?' It is typical of the difference between ancient and modern idiom that we, when we want to complain that a situation has grown intolerable, never say 'How long?' Therefore, when a Hebrew author writes 'How long, O Lord, wilt thou be angry?' you have to translate, 'What, Lord, art thou still angry?'—or perhaps, 'Lord, wilt thou never cease to be angry?' Literally translated into English, the Hebrew loses its force; it could not be otherwise. A hundred turns of phrase confront you as you read the Old Testament which make you sit back in your chair and ask yourself, 'What would an Englishman have said?'

When I say 'an Englishman', I do not mean a modern Englishman. The Old Testament record is of events that happened a very long time ago, under primitive conditions; to strike a note of modernity in rendering it is to make fun of it. The new Catholic version of Genesis which has just appeared in the States contains one such lapse into the vernacular. When Eleazar, Abraham's steward, has gone to Mesopotamia to find a wife for Isaac, this version represents him as 'waiting to learn whether or not the Lord had made his trip successful'. Now, I am not objecting to that as an American way of talking. My objection is that an American would not speak of the Mormons as having had a successful trip to Salt Lake City in A.D. 1850. All the less should they speak of Eleazar as having had a successful trip in 1850 B.C. A successful trip suggests shifting your cigar from one side of your mouth to the other as you alight from your aeroplane in San Francisco. It does not suggest trekking over miles of desert on a camel. You cannot do justice to antiquity without taking refuge in rather old-fashioned English. A Biblical phrase like 'O King, live for ever!' has got to be changed; nobody ever talked like that in English. But you must not change it into 'I hope that your Majesty's life may be spared indefinitely'. You must get back to the language of a period when palace etiquette was more formal, 'Long life to the King's majesty!'—something like that.

This is not meant to be a complete list of the difficulties which beset, as I see it, the path of the conscientious translator. Believe me, I have only indicated a handful of them. I have only attempted a partial answer to the question which naturally suggests itself to the un-initiated: 'What, nine years to translate the Bible! Fancy taking as long as that!'

# VII

## MORSU AMARISSIMO

I COULD not resist the quotation; but indeed it is inapplicable. When Dr. Bird was kind enough to notice, in *The Tablet*, my efforts to produce a rendering of the new Latin Psalter, he showed a scholar's generosity in making allowance, as far as he might, for the shortcomings of the amateur. If, on a first reading, I found myself murmuring the familiar lines:

> Perhaps it was right to dissemble your love,
> But why did you kick me downstairs?

further reflection reminded me that praise from Dr. Bird, though it be incidental, is praise worth having. And he is complimentary beyond all I deserve, if only I would stick to my *métier*. Never was so sugar-coated an atom-bomb.

Whether the publishers would have been better advised to put out a word-for-word translation of the new Psalter, it is not for me to determine. But I think they understood that if I tried my hand at it, the result would be a cock-shy—or, if you will, a pilot-engine to explode the booby-traps that await my Old Testament efforts. When I brought out a version of the New Testament, it first appeared in a privately printed form, welcoming criticism; and the generous response of the public to this appeal enabled me to introduce some five hundred alterations into the authorized edition. This in spite of previous overhauling by a committee of experts—Dr. Bird was one. My Old Testament rendering has undergone no such preliminary scrutiny; all the more welcome, then, is criticism of its character from Dr. Bird or from anybody else who is kind enough to read it. There are bound to be mistakes in it, faults of taste, exaggerations.

A cock-shy—and God forbid I should grudge Dr. Bird his coconuts. His scholarly instinct will have detected, from internal evidence, one uncomfortable fact, namely that my rendering is not, as a matter of history, a rendering from the new Roman text. It is a rendering from the Vulgate, corrected over the top so as to suit the requirements of the new Roman text. Not of my own choice, the process of correction was done in a hurry, and sometimes, through inadvertence, the original typescript has been left unamended. I am grateful to Dr. Bird for calling my attention to three such passages, v. 12, xv. 2, and xlix. 11. *Habet confitentem reum.*

But Dr. Bird's quarrel with me is not when I fail in what I am attempting to do; it is when I succeed. Precisely where I satisfy my own standards of translation, I cease to satisfy his. Nor, I am glad to say, will his candid temper allow him to throw out a vague charge of 'paraphrase', and leave it at that. He has collected a set of instances to illustrate his thesis that 'paraphrase and interpretation may lead us far away from the Latin', and invites the reader to 'decide for himself'. He does not say whether he regards them as typical or as salient instances; whether they are just a fair sample, or the pick of the bunch. But I know well—*et ego in Alexandria vixi*—how hard it is at the last moment to lay your hand on that particularly glaring passage where the other fellow did *really* give himself away. No doubt Dr. Bird has 'twenty-nine distinct damnations, one sure if another fails'; but he has only put down nine on the charge-sheet, and I must be content with those. To comment even on a handful of texts will be to indicate the line of defence on which I would urge the reader to take a lenient view.

(i) *Servite Domino in timore et exsultate ei ; cum tremore praestate obsequium illi, ne irascatur et pereatis de via* (ii. 11, 12). 'Tremble, and serve the Lord, rejoicing in his presence, but with awe in your hearts; kiss the rod, do not brave the Lord's anger and go astray from the sure path.' It will be noticed at once that I have deserted the punctuation of the new Latin text. But I am assured by a Scriptural expert that it would be a new departure if a particular punctuation of Holy Writ were prescribed with any binding force; and since nothing has been said, I am hardy enough to transpose the comma and the semicolon. *Praestate obsequium illi* is not the simple thing it looks, and I wonder whether I am the person who has been paraphrasing? The Greek has 'grasp instruction tight'; hence our old *apprehendite disciplinam*. But the Hebrew has 'kiss the son', or (if that can be made to mean anything) 'kiss sincerely'. Some ingenious person has suggested that the Psalmist wrote 'kiss his feet', and a note appears to indicate that the compilers of the new version adopt this reading. But they do not translate *osculamini pedes eius*, as you would expect; why? Presumably because they dislike the idea of basing an authoritative rendering on a scholar's guess. So they paraphrase. They give you a rendering which quite certainly is not a word-for-word rendering of what the Psalmist wrote; they give you a general idea of submissiveness, and leave it at that. Now, we have an excellent English way of putting that, 'kiss the rod'; it preserves the word 'kiss', which quite certainly is in the Hebrew, and links up the sense with the *virga ferrea* of verse 9. It was not a temptation I could resist.

After that, the sentence wants breaking up; we mustn't have people calling our sentences 'clumsy'. And we must avoid the change of subject inside a dependent clause, which makes awkward English. Thus 'lest he be angry and you get lost out of the path' becomes 'do not brave his anger and go astray from the path'. The *Dominus* of the old version was left in by mistake; I am delighted to get rid of it. The 'sure' path I kept on purpose, not so much because there is a lot to be said for the Greek reading here (cf. Briggs, ad loc.) as because it sounds better and adds, in reality, nothing to the sense.

(ii) *Deducit me per semitas rectas propter nomen suum.* 'By sure paths he leads me, as in honour pledged' (xxii. 3). *Semita recta* is not, I think, a dead-straight line; no guidance is needed to show a man that; it is the road that gets you there safely (I Esdras viii. 21; Jer. xxxi. 9). What is meant by 'for thy name's sake'? The ordinary Bible-reader thinks, wrongly, that it is a kind of vague adjuration. It means, throughout the Old Testament, 'because otherwise thy reputation will suffer (as being unable to afford thy promised protection)'. To reduce that to short compass, and soften down slightly what seems to us a bargaining tone, I have written, 'as in honour pledged'.

(iii) *Attollite, portae, capita vestra, et attollite vos, fores antiquae, ut ingrediatur rex gloriae.* 'Swing back, doors, higher yet; reach higher, immemorial gates, to let the King enter in triumph' (xxiii. 7). Let the reader, before he condemns me, ask himself what picture this verse conjures up in his mind? 'The ancient doors,' says Delitzsch, 'are to open themselves high and wide.' Yes, tell a door to swing itself wide, and we all see at once what is meant; but there is nothing here about swinging *wide* at all. The doors are to 'lift up their heads', and it is no use translating 'lintels' instead of 'heads'; how on earth can a door lift up its own lintel? Lifting up one's head is plainly a Hebraism for becoming higher; which suggests to me the figure of some great door (of a College, for instance) with a smaller opening cut away at the bottom, which admits the ordinary visitor; on state occasions the whole door must be opened, from ground to arch. I may have got the wrong impression, but at least I have got an impression; has anybody else? 'Immemorial gates' gives the meaning of the Hebrew 'gates of eternity'; then why not change 'King of glory' into 'triumphant King' or its equivalent? The word 'of' in English inevitably suggests that glory is the realm over which the king rules, and that is certainly not the intention of the Hebrew.

(iv) *Bonus et rectus est Dominus, propterea peccatores edocet viam.* 'How gracious is the Lord, how faithful, beacon-light of sinful souls' (xxiv. 8). Yes, I am inclined to think I have put too much into that; 'guide' would have been enough, without trying to be over-picturesque. Thank you, Dr. Bird.

(v) *Et dilatant contra me os suum; dicunt: Vah! Vah! oculis nostris vidimus!* 'See how they mop and mow at me, crying out, Joy, joy that we should have lived to see this!' (xxxiv. 21). The translator of the Old Testament is always being held up by the differences between Jewish gesture and ours. We hiss in disapproval, but not in derision or in astonishment; we slap our thighs at the dawning of a new light on our minds, not in agonized grief, and so on. An Englishman making faces at an unpopular figure does not 'open his mouth wide'. But the dictionary gives a quotation 'drawing her mouth an inch and a half wider than ordinary, and mopping at him', and 'to mop and mow' is good Byron. I think it will have to stand. 'Joy, joy!' is good Moore, and though I am not fond of it, I cannot better it. Why not 'Aha! Aha!' asks

Dr. Bird, or 'Well done, well done!'? But 'Aha!', outside Bible-English, is a form of roguish expostulation, not
of triumph; 'Well done!' implies a performer, and who
is the performer in question here? I notice that Dr. Bird,
in his own translation, gives, 'Vah! Vah! Our eye hath
seen', but does this *mean* anything? The Hebrews talked
of 'seeing' in the sense of gloating over a spectacle; our
nearest equivalent is 'living to see the day' when some
desirable thing happens.

(vi) *Rivus Dei repletus est aquis, parasti frumentum eorum;
ita enim parasti eam.* 'From that deep channel whence thy
divine ordinance provides our human needs' (lxiv. 10).
I hope Dr. Bird is not objecting to 'channel'; the new
Psalter, in correcting *flumen* to *rivus*, has given *peleg* its
true pipe-line significance. For the rest, the verse is
utterly obscure. 'Thou hast fixed up their [whose?] corn,
for so [how?] thou hast fixed it [what?] up.' Must we
interpret it as a hopeless tautology, 'Thou dost fix up
their corn, for it is by fixing it up that thou doest fix it
up'? ('Corn,' too, is masculine, and 'it' feminine.) Or
must we interpret it as a pointless antithesis, 'Thou dost
fix up their corn, for it is by fixing up the corn that thou
dost fix up the earth'? No wonder if the more unscrupu-
lous editors reject the last clause as dittography; no wonder if the Prayer-book version, by a heroic paraphrase,
gives the rendering 'for so thou providest for the earth'.

The compilers of the Authorized Version rightly saw
that the channel has got to be connected with its sur-
roundings, instead of being sealed off at both ends, if you
are to get a real translation; '(thou greatly enrichest it)
*with* the river of God *which* is full of water'; I have
imitated them. 'Of God' sins against the principle that,
in an English sentence, the same subject cannot be
alluded to both in the second and in the third person;

hence 'divine'. But 'divine channel' will hardly stand;
the epithet must be deferred till later. It seems certain
that 'of them' refers to the human race in general,
although its grammatical antecedent is perhaps the
dwellers at the world's end, mentioned in verse 9. Since
all the rest of the psalm is in the first person plural, I have
tried to simplify matters by talking of 'our' human needs.
So much for the general strategy of the sentence; my
conscience is not so clear about having reduced the un-
translatable third clause to the single word 'ordinance'.
Perhaps there is room for a fuller rendering; 'from yon-
der deep channel, divine source of our human nourish-
ment; such care thou hast for us', or something of that
kind.

(vii) *Deus assurgit in concilio divino, in medio deorum
judicium agit.* 'See, where he stands, the Ruler of all,
among the rulers assembled, comes forward to pro-
nounce judgement on the rulers themselves!' (lxxxi. 1).
The holy Angels are not in question here; the context
alone would warrant us in the belief that there was a
Hebrew usage which referred to human judges as 'gods'.
We have no such usage in English; consequently, the
translator is faced with a strict choice between paraphrase
and polytheism. I have chosen paraphrase. The new
Psalter's *concilio divino* allows for, without necessitating,
the interpretation 'assembly of God', i.e. Israel (Barnes).
In spite of the singular noun given by the Massoretic text,
this seems improbable; the rulers are not those of Israel,
but those of the surrounding nations (Briggs, Boylan).
The context shows that when Almighty God is represented as holding assize 'in the midst of' the rulers, they
are to be regarded not as his co-assessors but as prisoners
on their trial (cf. Ps. cix. 2).

(viii) *Nam illic, qui abduxerant nos, rogaverunt a nobis*

*cantica, et qui affligebant nos, laetitiam: Cantate nobis ex canticis Sion!* 'When the men who took us prisoner cried out for a song. We must make sport for our enemies; A stave, there, from the music they sing at Sion!' (cxxxvi. 3). Here I confess I rubbed my eyes, and looked about in some bewilderment for the cause of offence. My crime, I suppose, is to have used the word 'stave'; the kind of word Dr. Bird cannot endure, because it is not in common use among our contemporaries. But we are not discussing, here, proprieties of English usage; the complaint was that I had not translated the Latin. Have I not? The reader must decide for himself.

(ix) *Dominus bellator est: Dominus nomen eius.* 'Javé, the warrior God, Javé, whose very name tells of omnipotence!' (Cant. Mos. Ex. xv. 3). In a handful of instances I have felt it necessary to transliterate the Tetragrammaton; Jehovah to our ancestors, Yahweh to our contemporaries. I have made it into a Latin word, to match all the other names in the Old Testament; the Latins had no initial Y, and no W; they did not use H after a vowel. So I have written Javé, with an accent to deter the refectory reader from making it rhyme with 'brave'.

Yahweh is a name; 'the Lord' is a title. Or, rather, it is a religious euphemism; it dispenses you from the necessity of pronouncing a Name too holy to be pronounced. We have the same instinct in ordinary conversation; we avoid the Holy Name of Jesus, and substitute the title 'our Lord' instead. It would be perfectly conceivable to publish an edition of the New Testament which substituted 'our Lord' for 'Jesus' in most contexts: 'Then our Lord was taken up by the Spirit into the wilderness', and so on. But if we read, 'She will bear a Son, whom thou wilt call our Lord', the result would be grotesque. And it is equally grotesque to read, in the Old Testament, 'whose name is the Lord'. It is not a name, it is a title. Hence, in rare contexts like the present, I have preserved the Tetragrammaton.

But there is worse to follow. When you have said, 'Javé, whose name is Javé', you have not said anything. It is not even a tautology, it is a strictly identical judgement; and an identical judgement has no meaning at all except when idiomatically used. 'Eighty-two is eighty-two' has no meaning. 'Boys will be boys,' or 'East is East and West is West', means something because we are using an accepted English idiom; we are understood to mean that persons of immature age will behave in an immature manner, and so on. And evidently the Hebrews were using a Hebrew idiom when they uttered the apparent truism, 'Javé's name is Javé'. It is not difficult to see what kind of thing they meant. If someone used the words 'Our Holy Father Pope Pius XII; his name is Pius'; we should guess he meant that the Holy Father was a man of piety, true to his name. But it would not be an English idiom. Curiously (as so often) you can nearly match it from American slang; if an American says 'Discretion is my middle name' he is claiming to be, notoriously, discreet. But it is not English.

The translator, then, has to find a way of indicating, in English, that the God who is called Javé possesses the qualities which that name implies. To the Englishman there is nothing in a name; a rose by any other name would smell as sweet; but to the Jew it is *nomen et omen*, it implies the presence of qualities. Traditionally, of course, Yahweh implies eternity first and foremost; Reuss translates it, invariably, 'l'Éternel'. But the Vulgate Latin seems to take a different view; avoiding, most unexpectedly, the tautology of the original, it gave us

*Dominus quasi vir pugnator; omnipotens nomen eius*, as if to suggest that omnipotence was what the name Yahweh implies. I translated accordingly, 'Javé, whose very name tells of omnipotence'.

The new Psalter, true to its word-for-word principle, substituted *Dominus* for *Omnipotens*, and the formally identical judgement returned to us. What was I to do? Write 'Dominance' over the top instead of 'Omnipotence'? Or replace it by 'Eternity'? On the whole, I decided to leave the verse as it was. The significance of a name need not depend, after all, on mere etymology; a name may imply any quality that is habitually associated with it. And for sixteen centuries the *ecclesia orans* had been associating the Divine name with omnipotence. One thing I could not bring myself to do—inform the casual English reader that the Lord's name is the Lord.

'It was the wish of the Supreme Pontiff,' Dr. Bird reminds us, 'that the new Latin translation should combine a faithful rendering of the original texts with a careful regard, as far as possible, for the venerable Vulgate and the ancient versions. How far this faithful rendering can be preserved in a paraphrastic translation is open to question.' I know, but who said anything about preserving it? An artist is about to paint my portrait; he asks me to send him a photograph. I sit to Messrs. Bulbsqueezer, and implore them to produce a faithful likeness, to spare me nothing. Do I thereby lay it down that the artist's portrait must be indistinguishable from a coloured photograph? The new Latin Psalter was produced for the benefit of ecclesiastical persons, whose second mother-tongue is that Hebraeo-Roman dialect which we call 'ecclesiastical Latin'. In that dialect, naturally, the new Psalter was written; it would have been fantastic to write it in the idiom of Cicero or

Tacitus; the Romans are dead, and only a handful of scholars would have appreciated its flavours. Does it follow that when a vernacular translation is produced, for the English-speaking public at large, it must needs be written in the Hebraeo-Romano-Britannic dialect which I call 'Bible-English'? Must the common Englishman be forbidden to share the aspirations of King David, clothed in living language, because Dr. Bird would have done it otherwise?

But I must return to wrestling with Zachary. *His plagatus sum in domo eorum qui diligebant me.* . . .

# VIII

# FAREWELL TO MACHABEES

As the traveller, lost in some impenetrable jungle, and convinced that he will never make his way out of it alive, sits down to blaze on a tree-trunk the record of his wanderings, for the benefit of some luckier explorer in times to come; so the translator, seeing the end before him of a task which can never be complete, is fain to draw breath, to look round him, and to meditate on the reflex principles which have guided him thus far. Dr. Goodspeed, leaving the Old Testament to be finished by an indifferent team of collaborators, went straight on from the Apocalypse to his *Problems of New Testament Translation*. And shall not I, with Heliodorus' quip still ringing in my ears, be pardoned if I take time off to watch my own proceedings? Not, heaven knows, in the hope of disarming my critics; but with the more modest ambition of satisfying the unprejudiced onlooker who asks, in no unkind spirit, what exactly I think I am getting at.

A division of the subject readily presents itself. Your examination of conscience, when you are doing any translating work, is obviously grouped under three heads: Is it accurate? Is it intelligible? Is it readable? When you are dealing with the Old Testament, those three hurdles form a perspective of increasing difficulty.

(i) *To be accurate*, in rendering any passage of the Old Testament, you have to be perpetually exercised over the exact meaning of Hebrew words (and, consequently, of their Latin token-equivalents) which have been rendered inexactly ever since the time of Coverdale. I have already tried to explain[1] how difficult it is to find a satisfactory substitute for 'justice'. But it is not only 'justice' that has no exact equivalent in English; most of the commonest words in the Old Testament, if you give them their traditional values, are nearly always a point or so out of the true. *Nephesh* often means 'appetite'; and elsewhere it nearly always means 'life' rather than 'soul'. *Shalom* is much more like 'health' than 'peace', and much more like 'prosperity' than either—I cannot remember Reuss ever rendering it by *paix*. *Emeth* is what we mean by 'loyalty' or 'honour', not what we mean by 'truth'. *Chesed* is almost any kind of goodness, and the Vulgate's *misericordia* is often misleading; with the adjective, matters are still worse. *Yeshuah* can be 'victory' as well as 'deliverance'. *'Am* does duty for 'army' as well as 'people'. And so on. Those of us who were brought up on the Authorized Version have got it firmly in our heads that there were three main types of occasional sacrifice, the meat-offering, the sin-offering, and the peace-offering. But the whole point of the 'meat-offering' was that it consisted entirely of vegetable food; the 'sin-offering' arose, commonly, from a fault of inadvertence; and whatever the 'peace-offering' was exactly, editors seem agreed that it had nothing to do with peace. Always you are conscious of trying to open a door with a key that doesn't quite fit.

Of course, there are occasions where the Latin differs deliberately from our present Hebrew text, as when St. Jerome insists on making the skies rain down a Just Man, instead of justice; in such a passage as 'I know that my Redeemer liveth' you have no course open but to desert the Hebrew. There are occasions, too, where the

[1]See pp. 29-34.

Latin is almost certainly a mistaken attempt to render the Hebrew we have got, and you must put things right by elaborate footnotes. But worse still is the steady pull of the Latin token-words against the unmistakable meaning of the original. And this creates an especial difficulty, because so many chance phrases of the Old Testament have been encrusted in the Liturgy, and often in a false perspective. *O quam pulchra est casta generatio cum claritate*; the words have got to be used every time we celebrate a virgin's feast. But they have nothing to do with virginity; they are an attempt to console people who die childless. Are you to keep the meaning of the original in its true setting? Or are you to desert the original and preserve the liturgical overtones? The title *Sol justitiae* occurs in the Litany of the Holy Name; is one bound, in loyalty to the *Ecclesia orans*, to give the phrase a personal twist in Malachy iv. 2? It sounds all right, because the words are familiar, to talk about the Sun of Justice rising with healing in his wings. But the awkward fact is that Malachy says 'in *her* wings'; obviously he wouldn't have made *shemesh* feminine if he had been thinking of a personal theophany. The word 'his' occurs in our versions because it is pre-Jacobean English for 'its'.

You get the same trouble even with New Testament quotations. The word 'faith' expresses two different ideas, as entertained (consciously) by Habacuc and by St. Paul. Did Osee mean 'mercy' when he contrasted *chesed* with sacrifice (vi. 6)? Modern translators give you 'piety'; and it is quite possible that our Lord (Matt. ix. 13) was interpreting his thought. I confess that my New Testament quotations do not always tally verbally with their Old Testament originals. (But how can they? Cf. Eph. iv. 8). In a hundred ways, the vocabulary of Judaism shades off, by imperceptible gradations, into that of

Christianity. 'Life' to us means eternal life; to the Old Testament authors it meant, commonly at least, living to be a hundred. *Da mihi animas!* has been the slogan of much apostolic endeavour; yet Challoner did not hesitate to substitute 'Give me the persons' for Douay's 'Give me the souls' in Genesis xiv. 21; was he right? 'The spirit of the Lord'—how often you hesitate about printing, or not printing, a capital S! Douay gives you a capital in Isaias xi. 2, but in Challoner it is lower case. All your pious instincts make you want to emphasize, throughout the Old Testament, its half-conscious foreshadowing of the New. All your scholarly instincts make you want to reproduce the exact *nuance* of the eighth century B.C. To which of those instincts should the translator yield, if he wants to be 'accurate'?

Minor discrepancies between the Vulgate and the Hebrew, or between the Vulgate and modern commentators on the Hebrew, abound certainly, but are not of great significance. If the Vulgate tells me it means a hedge-hog and the commentators tell me it is a bittern, I am inclined to let St. Jerome have his way, as long as my naturalist friends inform me that the hedge-hog does really make a nest. The principle is the same; the loneliness of a ruin is underlined by the presence of shy animal life, whether of bitterns or of hedge-hogs. It would be otherwise if you translated from the Septuagint; in one passage, where the received text gives you 'a holy person' the Septuagint has 'hyena'. It seems the safest principle to follow the Latin—after all, St. Jerome will sometimes have had a better text than the Massoretes— except on the rare occasions when there is no sense to be extracted from the Vulgate at all. You cannot, I think, be tied down to the statement that Saul was one year old when he came to the throne, merely because that is the construction which the Vulgate has put on an obviously defective Hebrew original.

(ii) *To be intelligible* when you are translating a document, it is not enough to produce a series of sentences, each of which, taken by itself, has a meaning. You have got to show the argument running through your piece, or you have not fulfilled your contract; you have not translated.

There are some sentences, even in the Authorized Version, which must be pronounced unintelligible. My favourite one is Amos iv. 2 and 3: 'The Lord God hath sworn by his holiness, that, lo, the days shall come upon you, that he will take you away with hooks, and your posterity with fish-hooks, and ye shall go out at the breaches, every cow at that which is before her, and ye shall cast them into the palace, saith the Lord'. The translator who shows up that kind of thing must not be allowed to get away with it. The sulky schoolboy's defence, 'Well, that's what it says', is no defence at all. He must be sent back to his place and told to do better. There are not many sentences like that in the Authorized Version; sentences, I mean, which make no impact on the mind. In the Douay they are regrettably common; a verse like 'Shall not the land tremble for this and every one mourn that dwelleth therein, and rise up altogether as a river, and be cast out, and run down as the river of Egypt?' is just an ordinary verse in the Douay, not a museum piece. But a non-significant verse like that, here and there, is no great matter; you can pick up the thread again, if there is a thread to pick up. The trouble is that so often the thread itself is lacking.

Cut the Old Testament in half, at the end of Esther, and you may say that all the first half is intelligible, being either historical narrative, or legal enactments. There are difficult passages, to be sure, like the specifications for building the Tabernacle, or the Temple. But you know where you are all the time. The second half contains Machabees, which is narrative again; contains the Psalms, Proverbs and Ecclesiasticus, in which you do not expect, from the nature of the case, a continuous argument. All the rest of Part II, except Daniel and Jonas, is unintelligible unless you can translate it, not verse by verse, but chapter by chapter (or at least section by section) so that it makes an impression on the reader's mind. Has it, in fact, been so translated? Take the rattling of forks in the refectory for your answer.

The book of Job is a sustained piece of forensic pleading; the subject under debate being, Whether misfortunes are, in every case, a divine punishment for some fault wittingly or unwittingly committed? Nobody would claim that Job and his friends stick to the point with complete relevance; their own rhetoric carries them away. But the argument is going on all the time; and a good translation ought to be such that, running your eye down a few verses, you can see which side is arguing, without having to look up the rubric. Whether such a translation can be done, I don't know; I am very far indeed from feeling that I have done it. But in so far as you fail, the book of Job ceases to be what it was meant to be, a philosophical dialogue, and becomes a collection of purple patches, mainly about natural history.

Ecclesiastes and Wisdom are also philosophical arguments, though not in the form of dialogue. The former is comparatively easy, but you have to watch your step all the time, or you find yourself missing the emphasis and therefore losing the thread. Wisdom is so difficult that I toyed with the idea of writing a thesis to prove it was written by St. Paul, still unconverted. It is largely an appeal to past history, but for some reason the author prefers to write history without using any proper names. Quite certainly, it is the office of the translator to put them in, when their absence make the allusions intolerably obscure.

With the Canticle of Canticles, we are on more debatable ground. Some critics (Reuss, for instance, who was not a fool) have maintained that there is no unity here, it is only a collection of love-ballads. But you are conscious of special pleading. No, if I were allowed to mark a lacuna in the text at one point (the Chariots of Aminadab, where *something*, surely, has gone wrong with the text), I would be prepared to put it on the stage tomorrow. To insert stage directions in a translation would clearly be vulgar; nor would all commentators agree about the division of the lines. But you want to handle it very carefully, and make your footnotes very lucid, if if you are to light up the intensely human document that is enshrined in all that reliquary of mystical interpretation.

And then, the prophets! Practically a quarter of the Old Testament, and yet, apart from Daniel and Jonas, hardly a chapter you can read with your feet on the fender. Here, there is no question of a logical sequence of thought, carefully worked out; the Spirit blows where he will, not abiding our question. Yet beware of holding, in defiance of St. Jerome himself, that the prophets spoke in ecstasy; you are *haeresi proximus*, that way lies Montanism. Evidently the prophets—even Zachary—expected their contemporaries to understand what they were talking about. Only, their contemporaries had the advantage of us; they knew where one prophecy ended and another began, knew the occasion on which each was delivered, and the full details of the situation which led up to it. For all this, the modern reader is at the mercy of a set

of commentators, who take fantastic liberties with the
text. They assume from the first that it has reached us in
the form of a broken-up jigsaw, and proceed to reas-
semble it; they make up their minds from the first what
the prophet's message is, and ring off, with dark allusions
to the Machabaean period, when he starts talking about
anything else. (What they never seem to allow for is a
*defective* text; and yet in real life a copyist is far more
likely to drop things out than to foist things in.)

You can, I think, trace a continuous structure of
thought in Jeremias and Ezechiel, Aggaeus and Malachy;
in Joel, too, if you could be quite certain whether the
invaders were Assyrians or locusts. Elsewhere, there are
such sudden alternations of threat and promise, hope and
fear; the dating of events is so uncertain, the grouping
of them so confused; there is so little to show whether
the punishment of the heathen and the restoration of
Israel will happen the day after to-morrow or a few centuries hence—perhaps the best you can do is to treat
your text as a series of prophetic fragments, and decide
as judiciously as you may where the breaks come. Your
lot as a translator will be all the happier, if you remain
unconvinced by those modern speculations about 'metre'
which have mapped out Hebrew prophecy in a pattern of
strophes and antistrophes—but let that pass.

That the prophets, translate them how you will, can
ever be easy reading, I neither believe nor pretend. I do
claim that you can do something, and are bound to do all
you can, towards making them less unintelligible. The
transition from one sentence to the next must be made
logically clear, even at the cost of introducing words
which are not there, but are implicit in the context.
Your vocabulary must be chosen, not so much by reference to the use of this or that word elsewhere in the Old

Testament, as by reference to the needs of this particular passage—token-words will not do. You must cast your sentences into a form which will preserve not only the meaning but the *rhetoric* of the original, or the flying wrack of imagery will pass you by.

(iii) *To be readable*—reader, have you ever tried to be readable? Ever tried to compile a document which people would read, not because they had to, but because they wanted to? There is not much point in being accurate and intelligible, if nobody is going to read you.

Or rather, I distinguish. You may translate the Bible, as you might translate a French book on atomic physics, for the sake of the *student*. Please God, there will always be earnest people, perhaps one Catholic in a thousand, who will *study* the Scriptures; but the reader and the student (II Mach. ii. 26) are different people. Where are the Catholic *readers* of the Bible? When did you last come across one of your friends with a Bible open in front of him? In old days, non-Catholics used to read the Bible as a devotional exercise, much as we said the rosary. That is all over; nobody of my age who assists at the public solution of a crossword can understand modern hesitations about the identity of Bildad the Shuhite, or Tiglath-Pileser. We are in an odd situation. Nobody reads the Bible; popes and bishops are always telling us we ought to read the Bible, and when you produce a translation of the Bible, the only thing people complain about is your rendering of the diminutive snippets that are read out in church on Sundays. 'Of course,' they add, 'the book is all right for *private reading*'—in a tone which implies that such a practice is both rare and unimportant.

To be sure, the Old Testament is not everybody's money—parts of it, anyhow. Nothing in the world is going to make Leviticus newsy. But I do not see that the translator has acquitted himself of his task until he has made Paralipomenon as good reading at Berners' Froissart, and Ecclesiasticus as racy as Florio's Montaigne. I am convinced that the thing can be done, however much my own efforts may have fallen short of the target. And I am convinced that the thing is worth doing; what reason have we to suppose that the Scriptures can only be edifying if they are approached by way of the British Museum?

One difficulty confronts you at the very outset; the whole Hebrew way of putting things is diffuse, whereas we, more and more, grow accustomed to terseness. A language which talks about 'the God of Abraham and the God of Isaac and the God of Jacob', so as to make it clear that Isaac and Jacob are in the genitive, encourages you in the habit of leaving nothing to the imagination. Nine times in the fifth chapter of Genesis we are told that such and such a patriarch 'begat sons and daughters'; is it legitimate to convey precisely the same information by adding the postscript, 'All these had other sons and daughters besides'? Even more leisurely is the progress of Numbers vii. Verses 12 to 89 describe the gifts made by the Israelites at the dedication of the Tabernacle; by verse 17 we have finished the inventory of Juda's contribution, a silver dish, a silver bowl, and so on—only to find that Issachar made precisely the same contribution, which is repeated in full, and so on all through the twelve tribes, up to verse 83. The remaining six verses are occupied with adding up the totals. Obviously the translator must not avail himself of the useful word 'ditto'. But is he bound to repeat exactly how much the dish weighed, exactly how much the bowl weighed, exactly how old the lambs were, every time? There is a great deal of 'The word of the Lord came unto me saying, Go and speak unto this people, and thus shalt thou speak unto them, saying, Thus saith the Lord'; you cannot omit these formulas, but can nothing be done to scale down the effect of them?

But all that is of secondary importance. What matters is that the Bible should speak to Englishmen not only in English words, but in English idiom. Any translation is a good one in proportion as you can forget, while reading it, that it is a translation at all. Do not be deceived when your friends tell you that they *like* Bible-English. Of course they do, reading or quoting a few sentences; there is a slow-moving thoroughness about it which conveys a sense of dignity—you get the same in an Act of Parliament. But if they would try to read a chapter on end, which they never do, it would rapidly become tedious, and the attention would begin to wander; why? Because they are reading a foreign language disguised in English dress. Just so, an indifferently translated French book gets you down; *en effet* is translated 'as a matter of fact' when it ought to be translated 'sure enough', and *d'ailleurs* is translated 'anyhow' when it ought to be translated 'if it comes to that'. Your interpreter is almost imperceptibly failing all the time to hit the nail exactly on the head.

Easy enough to notice, as most of the modern translators do, when there is some positive Hebraism to be avoided; when turns of phrase like 'into the hand of' or 'by the hand of' can easily be exchanged for normal English equivalents. It is a harder part of the translator's job to notice the negative effect produced by the absence of English mannerisms. Here is an interesting question you may put to an unsuspecting friend: 'Which is commoner in the Old Testament; the word *danger* or the

word *peril*?' You will find that 'peril' has it; the concordance tells you that it occurs once in the Old Testament (Authorized Version), whereas 'danger' does not
occur at all. 'Jeopardy' comes three times. Now, it is
nonsense to suppose that the Hebrew mind has no such
notion as danger; why is there no word for it? The
answer can only be, that in Hebrew you express the
same idea by a nearly-allied word which has to do duty,
also, for slightly different ideas; a word like 'affliction',
'tribulation' or 'trouble'. That means, that a good translation of the Old Testament will sometimes give you
'danger' or 'peril', where the stock translations give you
'affliction', 'tribulation' or 'trouble'; sometimes, where
the stock translations give you 'fear' or 'terror'. The
rendering which does not mention danger or peril jars
imperceptibly on the mind.

More often, the difference involved is not one of mere
vocabulary; it depends on the whole build of a language,
the whole strategy of its rhetoric. To take a single
example—your modern reader is impatient to know what
happened, whereas your ancient author likes to spin out
the story, and keep his audience in suspense. If A wants
to borrow money from B, the sort of sequel you get in
the Old Testament is, 'And B answered him, saying,
Yesterday and the day before, when the Lord brought
Israel out of Egypt, he commanded us that we should not
turn away from our brethren when they were in
need . . .' and so on and so on, leading up to a refusal
five verses later. What the modern reader wants is, 'But
B refused; Yesterday and the day before, he said . . .'
and so on. The translator may feel bound to give a literal
rendering; is it not his duty to preserve the integrity of
a literary monument? But his reader has switched on the
wireless.

Perhaps the subtlest irritant of all is the Hebrew habit of parallelism. I know I shall get into trouble for saying this. The Hebrews, I shall be told, when they wanted to write poetry, deliberately repeated themselves, in some such formula as *Et intonuit de caelo Dominus | Et Altissimus dedit vocem suam*. You must reproduce that exactly in English, or you will not give the reader any idea what Hebrew poetry was like. My version of the Psalms has been given bad marks for this; Fr. Gruenthaner complains that 'the lines are not printed to bring out the parallelism and remind the reader that he is dealing with lyric poetry in a metrical form'. And Mgr. Barton says, 'There is really no excuse for this attempt to ignore the metrical quality'. Now, if I were prepared to take up that challenge as a mere point of typography, so far from not having any excuse, I have the excuse of a paper-shortage. To print the supposedly 'poetical' parts of the Old Testament all broken up into lines, as the moderns do, increases your newsprint length by something like one page in ten. That is all very well, if you are publishing hand-books for students. But if you are doing a translation which is meant to be read, not studied, and hope, consequently, that it will have a wide sale, the waste of space becomes serious. Again, the student in his library is accustomed to deal with bulky volumes. But if you hope that your translation will be handled on 'buses and in bed, you do not want to saddle the reader with extra weight. There is no harm, now and again, in being practical.

But I will come clean; I have tried, in great part, to obliterate the traces of parallelism, not merely in the printing of my translation, but in the writing of it. I quite understand people like Fr. Gruenthaner and Mgr. Barton, who are concerned with students, wanting to concentrate attention on the technical lay-out of Hebrew poetry. But what the reader wants, I insist, is to get the illusion that he is reading, not a translation, but an original work written in his own language. And to our notions of poetic composition, these remorseless repetitions are wholly foreign; when you have read a page or two on end, they begin to cloy. *Ars est celare artem*, and I have been at pains, not seldom, to conceal the art of my original. Thus, Isaias lx. 4 reads (in a modern translation):

'Your sons shall come from far,
And your daughters shall be borne on the hip'.

Obviously, the sex-discrimination is not intended; the older children, boy or girl, would walk, the little ones, girl or boy, would be carried. You want, therefore, something different; if you were translating from the Hebrew (the Vulgate necessitates a departure from it), you would write: 'Sons of yours, daughters of yours, come from far away; carried at their mothers' sides they come'. It is quite true, that does not show the working of the Hebrew sentence; but why should it? You are not mugging the thing up for an exam; you want to read the kind of thing an Englishman would write, if he were encouraging a modern set of Displaced Persons with the promise of restoration.

'Modern'—I have a confession to make. When I embarked on the Old Testament, I thought I could treat it as I treated the New; aim at a sort of timeless English that would reproduce the idiom of our own day without its neologisms, and perhaps have something of an old-fashioned flavour about it. The further I got into the Old Testament, the more surely it was borne in on me that you could not (as they say) swing it. The New Testament was new, the Old Testament was old. The New Testament was written, mainly, by people who thought in

Aramaic and used Greek as a kind of Esperanto; it has not the vigour of a living language. The Old Testament was written, mainly, by people who were using their own tongue, and expressed themselves naturally in it. A different treatment was called for, or the whole thing went desperately flat. What opened my eyes, I think, was a rendering by Reuss of the phrase, *Nigra sum sed formosa*. He went at it in a business-like way, as the French do, and produced '*Je suis brunette, mais je suis jolie*'.

'*Je suis brunette, mais je suis jolie*'—yes, it is all right, there is no slang there, no neologism, and yet. . . . It is not, somehow, the Canticles. Or take that very pains-taking piece of work, the Old Testament companion to Goodspeed. Nahum ii. 9 reads:

'Plunder silver, plunder gold;

For there is no end to the stores,

An abundance of all sorts of valuable articles'.

Marked out in lines, you see, to give the poetical effect; but *does* it give a poetical effect? Nahum has disappeared, and you are left with the language of a cloak-room notice. You cannot make your rendering into poetry by just chopping it up into lengths.

No, what is needed, if we are ever to have a first-class translation of the Old Testament, is a return to the past; to an earlier and more vigorous tradition of English, such as the old translators had, Florio, and North, and Holland, and Urquhart, and L'Estrange, and Adlington. They really managed to 'English' the classical and foreign authors they dealt with, because their own language was still fluid, and could adapt itself to shades of thought; it was not yet cast into a mould. I say 'if we are ever to have a first-class translation'; that is not mock-modesty about my own efforts. I seriously doubt whether I have had the courage or the skill to go back, sufficiently, to those old models. But I have felt, all along, the impetus. Take the book of Proverbs, for example; why does it all read so flat? Because your Hebrew author always writes at full length, whereas the English tradition is to reduce the aphorism to a minimum of words. 'As the cold of snow in the time of harvest, so is a faithful messenger to them that send him'—that is not English; the Englishman says, 'Faithful messenger, harvest snow', and leaves it at that.

May I give a single, short example, to illustrate the kind of problem I have been discussing? In the Authorized Version, slightly more lucid as usual than the Douay, the 65th chapter of Isaias begins as follows:

'I am sought of them that asked not for me; I am found of them that sought me not; I said, Behold me, behold me, unto a nation that was not called by my name. I have spread out my hands all day unto a rebellious people, which walketh in a way that was not good, after their own thoughts.'

At first sight, it would appear that verse 1 refers to the call of the Gentiles, verse 2 to the rejection of Israel; and this allegorical interpretation is put on the passage in Romans x. 20. But modern editors are agreed that the Massoretic text is wrongly pointed; LXX and Vulgate are right in giving 'that did not call upon my name' at the end of the sentence. And they are agreed that verse 1, no less than verse 2, refers to the rejection of Israel. The point throughout is that God made himself available to the Jews; if you may put it in that way without irreverence, he was like a grown-up playing hide-and-seek with his favourite children, peeping out from his hiding-place and making their task of search fool-proof, only to find that they had got tired of the game, and were not looking for him at all. In the context, that is to say, verse 1 means something wholly different from what the older versions tell you; they are inaccurate, because they are over-literal. How to correct the inaccuracy? This was my first attempt, made several years ago, when I was new to the job:

'I let myself be questioned by men who do not begin by asking for me; I let myself be found by men who do not search for me; it is to a nation which never calls on my name that I say, I am here, I am close at hand. All day long I spread out my hands to a rebellious people, that goes astray in following its own devices; a people that is ever openly defying me.'

I claim, here, some merit for ingenuity. You can read verse 1 so as to make it apply, in St. Paul's way, to the Gentiles; you can also read it so that it will apply to the Jews, and lead on naturally to verse 2. The rendering is accurate, and just intelligible. But what a rendering! How is anybody going to read through sixty-six chapters of Isaias, all Englished in so stilted and so pedantic a fashion? I might ask the printer to make good my short-comings:

'I let myself be questioned
    By men who do not begin by asking for me;
I let myself be found
    By men who do not search for me'—

no doubt I could sell my shoddy goods with a little window-dressing like that; Fr. Gruenthaner would be delighted. But is it worth it?

This is how the passage stands at present:

'So ready I to answer, and ask they will not; so easy to be found, and search for me is none! A people that will not call upon my name; else my own voice should whisper, I am here, I am close at hand! Outstretched these hands of mine, all the day long, to a nation of rebels, straying this way and that as the mood takes them, openly defying me.'

That is its present form; I do not say, its final form; nearly all this process of revision has been done in railway trains. But I hold to it that you have got to do something *of that kind* if you want to let the reader into the mind of Isaias.

*Legentibus, si semper exactus sit sermo, non erit gratus.* I wonder where St. Jerome found that thought-provoking sentiment to end Machabees with? It is not in the Greek.